Reflected Love

Reflected Love

Companioning in the Way of Jesus

CHRISTOPHER BROWN

WIPF & STOCK · Eugene, Oregon

REFLECTED LOVE
Companioning in the Way of Jesus

Wipf & Stock
An Imprint of Wipf and Stock Publishers
199 W. 8th Ave., Suite 3
Eugene, OR 97401
www.wipfandstock.com

ISBN 13: 978-1-62032-0051
Manufactured in the U.S.A.

To my wife Marilyn, companion along the way.

Contents

Come to me, all you that are weary and are carrying heavy burdens, and I will give you rest. Take my yoke upon you, and learn from me; for I am gentle and humble in heart, and you will find rest for your souls. For my yoke is easy, and my burden is light.[1]

---

1. Matt 11:28–30, *NRSV*.

Preface

A BOUT FIFTEEN years ago, I wrote a reflection on the first four Beatitudes from a position of close proximity to friends who had experienced serious mental illness.[1] As I immersed myself in the stories of my friends while at the same time engaging with Jesus' teaching, I discovered how the gospels—and all Scripture—enliven the contexts in which we are planted, since Jesus' teaching not only transforms the pilgrims of the gospel pages, but it also transforms us. Engaging with the Beatitudes, I realized that significant walls were within me—not just my friends—and Jesus was inviting both of us to attend to their dismantling.

As I began to introduce these gospel encounters with Jesus into personal reflections on my practice and also in my teaching, supervision, and formation work, my context, or "praxis," became more and more alive. By engaging in everyday human experiences, including places of pain, suffering, and death, Jesus manifested his life-giving and restorative purpose in the world, gifting us with a wealth of stories, images, and metaphors that keep us searching for more of his way. Most of my classes now begin with a reflection on a gospel encounter or a psalm, and participants can enter them in ways which bring them far closer to their

1. This was published in a small discussion paper entitled, "Dismantling the walls that divide." Brown, *Zadok Paper S78,* 1–14.

own lived experience than can pastoral care and counseling theory, important as these are.

As these reflections found their way into workbooks for students, I began to wonder if it was time to offer a more comprehensive book that might inspire interpersonal ministers to walk more deeply with pilgrims while also engaging more intimately with Jesus as their guide and mentor.

Over the past decade and a half, these insights have become foundational to my practice, supervision, and teaching in the field of interpersonal helping, which I refer to throughout this book as "companioning." As I have engaged with the gospel accounts of Jesus journeying with pilgrims towards inner healing and revelation, I have come to see that Jesus does not offer a program, method, practice theory or series of steps, but invites us, through his self-giving, other-receiving, and sacrificial love, to indwell his person and to be transformed into his likeness. Though formation in the likeness of Christ is our basic faith priority, it is often neglected in our interpersonal ministry training and development. Moreover, though many faith-committed interpersonal workers would acknowledge Jesus as the Master Therapist, not all would explore his life-giving way as much as they would contemporary theory and method. It is important to constantly remind ourselves, that in speaking of the deeper life of pilgrims and what it is to be human, "we have not said enough until we speak of God."[2]

In our interpersonal work, as we journey with people into their experiences, life events, crises, pains, joys, and sorrows, the Holy Spirit will gift us with the life, truth, and way of Jesus, empowering us to embody and reflect these

2. Laird, *Into the Silent Land*, 9.

gifts to those with whom we walk.[3] By reinstating Jesus, and indeed the community of the Trinity, right into the centre of our companioning, we can extend a relational space to burdened and oppressed pilgrims, where their worried-filled and overwhelming stories might come to a place of rest and safe communion with their Creator. Speaking for his Father in Heaven, Jesus said:

> Come to me, all you that are weary and are carrying heavy burdens, and I will give you rest. Take my yoke upon you, and learn from me; for I am gentle and humble in heart, and you will find rest for your souls. For my yoke is easy, and my burden is light.[4]

These words of Jesus offer us a window through which we can explore what Jesus is doing in his encounters with people and how he is going about it. This book uses this window to bring people involved in personal ministries as close as possible to the life-giving dynamic that is found in the person of Jesus and in his way of ministering. His 'Come to me . . . ' invites us into the flow of self-giving love—the giving of self and the receiving of the other, which is at the relational heart of the Trinity.[5] Categorizing ministers as problem-solvers, advisors, classifiers of life's difficulties, or assistants to troubled pilgrims falls short of Jesus' transformative and restorative purposes in the world and sidelines

3. John 14:6.

4. Matt 11:28–30, *NRSV.*

5. Volf, *Exclusion and Embrace,* 127.

his invitation for our active participation in the renewing of his kingdom on earth.[6]

But these words of Jesus also raise many questions, such as:

- How does this work out in the relationship we might offer a pilgrim?

- Can we really invite a person who is overwhelmed and in pain to a place of rest?

- What is it to offer a gentle and humble heart for the journey?

- Can we actually journey with people towards a place that offers real and substantial rest for the soul?

- Is Jesus really inviting us as companions to "become" his "invitation" and to extend the flow of the self-giving and other-receiving love of the Triune God to the pilgrims with whom we walk?

In this book, we will interact with these questions as we move closer to Jesus, our mentor and master guide-companion, by engaging with the gospels and considering how we might embody his life and reflect his restorative way in the work of companioning. The book is structured around four main companioning stories: Carol Compton's story in chapter three, Sandra Stark's in chapter seven, David Davison's in chapter ten, and Marjorie Meyer's in chapter eleven. These companioning stories are composites, in that they bring into single accounts experiences that have occurred in many different encounters.

6. Rom 12:2; Eph 4:23.

For us as companions, as for those to whom we offer guidance, coming to know the fullness of the person of Jesus also means coming to know ourselves, an unfolding discovery from the inside-out. As a companion and guide, Jesus is not foreign to us, because through him we were created and given life. Deep within the sanctuary of our soul we know his voice.[7] To draw close to him is to encounter the giving and receiving flow of God's Spirit, where we are fully loved, fully known, and invited to participate in his life and vocation.

Little-by-little, as his light illuminates our innermost being, Jesus leads us from ordinary, everyday levels of awareness towards inner revelation, calling us to wake up, look, listen, and learn. In this book we will refer to this call towards wakefulness as "attentiveness." Always sensitive to our unique history and capacity for growth, Jesus mirrors back to us how we can be reconciled—brought from fragmentation, disunity, and disconnection into unity, wholeness, holiness, and communion—as his humble, gentle, and wounded heart accompanies our divided and fearful hearts along this transformative life journey.

It has been wonderful to engage with so many people around these themes. In every group where we have reflected upon the companioning of Jesus, I have emerged with new insights and challenges, and so am myself in the ongoing process of becoming a companion in the gentle, loving, life-giving way of Jesus.

I wish to express my deep gratitude to the pilgrims who have joined me in the companioning room who, through being willing to reveal and attend to the deeper rhythms

7. John 10:14 & 16.

and flows of their lives, have enabled me to become witness to the transforming touch of Christ on the human soul. For well over a decade, staff at Christian Heritage College in Brisbane have invited me to work with groups of students around these themes, and more recently the college research group has provided financial assistance to bring this book to fruition.

I would especially like to thank Karen Hollenbeck Wuest, who as a gifted and committed editor, has taken a rambling manuscript, along with its core theme of the way of Jesus, into her life and heart, and companioned it through to readability and clarity.

There are my friends, the holy scribblers, Charles Ringma, Irene Alexander, and Terry Gatfield, who listened to roughly formed chapters and gave their ongoing encouragement and practical support. There is Patricia Nominson, who revealed to me a vital key to the companioning of Jesus, Sr. Juanita Scari RSJ, who mentored me in spiritual direction and encouraged me to be deeply attentive to the rhythms of grace in human experience, and my colleague Penny Box who helped me to work through these themes experientially with many groups of students. I am indeed grateful.

Finally, I would wish to acknowledge my wife Marilyn who graciously and lovingly companioned me through the lengthy gestations of this work in its many forms.

Christopher Brown
Currimundi, Queensland, Australia
January 2012

1

Passing Under the Low Lintel

Now as they went on their way, he entered a certain village, where a woman named Martha welcomed him into her home. She had a sister named Mary, who sat at the Lord's feet and listened to what he was saying. But Martha was distracted by her many tasks; so she came to him and asked, "Lord, do you not care that my sister has left me to do all the work by myself? Tell her then to help me." But the Lord answered her, "Martha, Martha, you are worried and distracted by many things; there is need of only one thing. Mary has chosen the better part, which will not be taken away from her."[1]

JESUS VISITS MARTHA AND MARY

In this gospel story from Luke, Jesus is welcomed across the threshold of Mary and Martha's home and comes into their world, humbly stooping to pass under "the low lintel" of their human hearts.[2] This story offers a noteworthy

---

1. Luke 10:38–42, *NRSV*.

2. Evelyn Underhill, from her poem, "Immanence." In Nicholson and Lee, *The Oxford Book*, No. 317.

1

entry point into the territory of pastoral care, counseling, and spiritual companioning, for after receiving his friends' welcome, Jesus welcomes them into his spacious presence, humbly fitting his stature to meet their needs,[3] while embracing them with his life-giving, restorative, and self-emptying way of love.[4]

Jesus' visit to this household brings his way close to us as he affirms the receptivity and responsiveness of Mary, and challenges the reactive and over-and-against energy of Martha. Both women are being invited to deeper life, where "there is the need of only one thing." In the passage that serves as our pilot guide for companioning, Jesus calls this "one thing" "rest for your souls."[5]

MARY SITS, JESUS INVITES

Sitting at the feet of Jesus, Mary is absorbed by Christ and what he is saying. This picture of openness and receptivity reveals Mary as one who is drawn into relationship with the life and light embodied within Jesus. His presence, his gentle, and humble heart, even more than his words, draws her to deeper levels of awareness and brings life to her soul. Prior to this occasion, might there have been a healing or inner transformation within Mary that has given her the self-assurance to set aside cultural, religious, and gender constraints, even to risk the ire of her sister, to come into the presence of Jesus and sit at his feet in this way?

3. Ibid.
4. Phil 2:7, Luke 4:18–19, John 6:33.
5. Matt 11:29.

Having chosen the "better part" does not suggest that Mary is more advanced in her faith journey than Martha, but reflects her receptivity to a relationship with Jesus, which enables her to move beyond the constraints that entangle Martha and so receive the gift of grace, the gift of divine presence, that Jesus is offering to her.[6] In this encounter between Mary and Jesus, we notice how Jesus holds both grace and truth in perfect unity. He does not need to exert influence or power over Mary because the desire for truth is already planted in her soul.[7] Through his manifest presence, Jesus beckons Mary to look at her everyday experience through the lens of spiritual awareness,[8] enabling her to see ordinary things in a new and profound way, and thus guiding her to a safe harbor where she can find rest for her soul.[9]

MARTHA REACTS, JESUS INVITES

The gospel encounter between Jesus and Martha portrays Martha in a reactive, over-and-against frame of mind. After welcoming Jesus as a guest, she becomes pre-occupied and distracted with her many hosting tasks. Martha's reactiveness comes to a head when she seeks to extend power over Mary by co-opting the influence of Jesus, her guest, to bring

6. 2 Peter 1:4.

7. John 1:14.

8. Cynthia Bourgeault helped me to see the levels of ordinary awareness, spiritual awareness and divine awareness contained within this gospel story (Luke 10:38–42). Bourgeault, *Centering Prayer*, 7–18.

9. Brother Lawrence, *The Practice of the Presence of God*, is a book offering many wonderful examples of this.

her sister into line: "Lord, do you not care that my sister has left me to do all the work by myself? Tell her then to help me."

In Jesus' masterful response, he brings into focus the events, experiences, and underlying emotions that are right in front of Martha in order to invite her to respond from a deeper place. He gently but firmly reflects back to Martha both her approach to her tasks and the emotional content that has entrapped her at the surface level of her life. He moves towards, not away from, Martha's experience, meeting her at her point of resistance and encouraging her to be attentive to what is happening inside. "Martha, Martha, you are worried and distracted by many things . . ." Then he names the shift from the many things to the "need of only one thing". Because Mary has been the target of Martha's projections, Jesus brings her back into the conversation, reaffirming his invitation to the deeper life he is offering: "Mary has chosen the better part, which will not be taken away from her."[10] Now Martha is invited to transformation, healing, and deeper life.

A careful examination of this encounter reveals that the relational space which Jesus opens for Martha is more significant than the words he uses. It is completely consistent with his "Come to me . . ."[11] That relationship is the bridge to the deeper life, to the one thing needed.[12] None of Martha's worries, entanglements, fears or projections find their counterparts in the person of Jesus, who is offering Martha a self-giving, self-emptying, and other-receiving

10. Luke 10:38–42, *NRSV*.

11. Matt 11:28.

12. Luke 10:32, *NKJV*.

love. The deepest cry emanating from within her fragile and wounded heart will painfully resonate within Jesus' gentle, humble, unprotected, and vulnerable heart.

The personal territory upon which this companioning encounter occurs is not neutral. If we step into this emotionally charged space, we might ask if Martha was really expecting Jesus to use his personal power to bring her sister into line. She was certainly putting something onto Jesus that he would need to decide whether or not to carry.

But Jesus had done his inner work well, including his unequivocal, "No" to the temptation of exercising power over others.[13] He knows that Martha will only grow into the fullness of her humanity by entering into the hospitable space, deeper life, and soul rest that he is offering through his presence, but he extends that relationship bridge in complete freedom.

THE COMPANION'S TASK AS ONE WHO TENDS THE STORY

While a religious teacher in the room of Mary and Martha's house might focus on the content of what Jesus was saying and how he was conveying this to his hearers, a spiritual companion would be more concerned about what was happening for Martha, Mary, and the others sitting near Jesus and what was beginning to stir within them. To companion is to enter the dynamics of the encounter between created beings and their Creator.

As I reflect on Mary's receptiveness, I remember the Mary's whom I have recently companioned. Each has re-

13. Matt 4:1–11.

sponded to my question, "What is it that is in front of you that would be useful to attend to in our time together?" with a pressing and troubling personal issue. By encouraging these women to attend closely the experience directly in front of them, they quickly moved into the regions of their hearts, looking in on themselves for new insights and understandings. In this place, each encountered warmth, love, and reaffirmation of her personhood as a child of God. Some sat in the embrace of the Divine Presence, while others inwardly danced or played. For some a verse of scripture emerged. From this place of safety, new and substantive responses emerged to the pressing issues that were in front of them, drawing them into the very midst of, rather than away from, the difficulties and pains of their lived experience, and there encountering the Divine. My companioning task was simply to keep each of these women attentive to what emerged in front of them as and when it surfaced.

I now take this prayerful reflection one step further by bringing these encounters together with our pilot passage, "Come unto me . . . and you will find rest for your soul . . ."[14] Notice how this is an invitation into relationship. In the context of this personal relationship, we are able to bring our weary and burdened selves, and the experiences that trouble us, into a place of rest. By opening his gentle and humble heart to us, Jesus draws us into the flow of love that moves between the Father and the Son, where we find this rest for our souls. The freedom of this relationship is that it does not involve heavy expectations or the exercise of power over us. In fact, Jesus concludes with, "For my yoke

14. Matt 11:28, 30, *NRSV*.

is easy, and my burden is light".[15] The challenge for me in my ongoing formation and growth is: "Which aspects of this relationship and this way might I be able to reflect and embody in my companioning?"

The women I companioned were certainly not sitting at my feet—in fact, they were sitting opposite. But I began to notice that as they moved into deeper levels of awareness, they were—like Mary—sitting at the feet of Jesus. Their personal encounter with the One who embodied the Good News for them was drawing them into deeper life and to the place of rest for their souls.

When I ponder where I might imaginatively locate myself in the encounter between Jesus and Mary, I see myself sitting with her some days later as she reflects on her time with her Lord, facilitating her reflection with questions such as: "What did you notice was happening for you as you sat at the feet of Jesus?" "If you were to look inside the person of yourself sitting at the feet of Jesus, what would you begin to notice?" "As you come to that place, what do you notice that invites your attention?"

Reflecting on my role as one who tends, or facilitates Mary's story, I see that I need to be in full cooperation with the Divine movement of grace and that my facilitation will need to reflect and embody the way of Jesus so that the shift from my companioning to that of Jesus will be as seamless as possible. I also acknowledge that Jesus' gift of the Holy Spirit will guide the whole encounter, recognizing that a vital part of my companioning task is to come into a more intimate relationship with Jesus, committed to do my own

15. Matt 11:30, *NRSV*.

inner work so that my whole person might be transformed into his likeness.

As we draw near to the feet of Jesus, our Master guide-companion, his light shines into our inner darkness, gently drawing our attention to the Martha within ourselves, thereby revealing any reactive entanglements and mixed motives that are filling us with over-and-against energy and constraining us to the narrow rim of our outer existence. As an icon of wholeness, freedom, and restoration, Jesus mends the residual disunity between our Mary and Martha parts, and it is this integrated, non-judgmental self that we seek to embody and reflect as we journey with other pilgrims.

Valuing each pilgrim's lived experiences, the companion creates a spacious place where the pilgrim can attend, gently and courteously, to her inner reverberations, so that her soul, in all its shyness, will reveal itself.

2

Living Beyond the Rim

He must increase, but I must decrease.[1]

CLEARING THE THRESHING FLOOR

A DESERT dweller nourished by a diet of locusts and wild honey,[2] John the Baptist preached a baptism of life-changing repentance and forgiveness of sins, preparing the way for the coming Messiah.[3] Having encountered God in his desert dwelling, he emerged free from personal, religious, and cultural entanglements. Dressed in rough camel hair with a leather belt around his waist, he drew crowds. Yet he could discern the hypocrites, who flocked to him for external cleansing, but did not want to be cleansed on the inside. Like the contemporary "wild man," John lived humbly out of the truth he spoke and had little regard for position and status,[4] an attitude that eventually led to his death.

1. John the Baptist speaking of Jesus. John 3:30, *NRSV*.
2. Matt 3:4; Luke 3:2, *MSG*.
3. Luke 3:3.
4. Luke 3:7–8.

9

We glimpse the inner freedom of John the Baptist when he announced the Messiah: "I baptize you with water for repentance, but One who is more powerful than I is coming after me; I am not worthy to carry his sandals. He will baptize you with the Holy Spirit and fire. His winnowing fork is in his hand, and he will clear his threshing floor and will gather his wheat into the granary; but the chaff he will burn with unquenchable fire."[5] Secure in his role as the first guide, sent to point towards the greater guide, John was willing to venture to truth's most dangerous cusp, where power can either respond and choose life or react and choose death.

With all the brilliance and freedom of the "wild man," John guides us to put our house in order, moving aside barriers and removing clutter, making the most of the space available to us until there is a semblance of internal order, readying us to welcome a significant guest. Yet the momentum does not remain with John, but points us towards Jesus, the greater guest and guide, who draws us to himself and offers us a life-giving flow of love with the Father.

LET IT BE SO NOW: ATTENDING TO WHAT IS NEEDED

The encounter between these two guides occurs at Jesus' baptism. Gazing through our companioning window to witness their exchange, we glimpse John preparing the way for Jesus by opening a sacred relational space. Ready to receive Jesus, John reveals a flicker of humble resistance when he says, "I need to be baptized by you, and do you come

5. Matt 3:11–12, *NRSV.*

to me?" Jesus responds receptively with, "Let it be so now," and is initiated into his full vocation.[6]

As Jesus emerges from that space, John sees God's Spirit descending upon him with the movement, lightness, and freedom of a dove. Along with the Spirit comes a voice, which expresses the profound relationship between Jesus and his Father: "This is my Son, the Beloved, with whom I am well pleased."[7]

Jesus extended this relational participation with the interflow of love between Father, Son, and Spirit to John when he asked him to baptize him. And Jesus extended that same life and light to the whole world[8] again when he willingly offered his abundant, overflowing life of grace and truth sacrificially on the cross.[9] When we open our hands to receive his fullness, wholeness, and holiness, through which "we have all received, grace upon grace,"[10] all of our human endowment seeks to praise and glorify our Creator. No longer people of the rim, fashioning our existence out of a frantic desire for safety, security, or exclusivity, we are returned again to the embrace of the Divine presence, in whom all the secrets of our origins, our experiences, and our destiny are safely and tenderly held.[11] With our minds enlightened and hearts strengthened, we walk as image bearers of our Creator, without fear, into the fullness of our vocation along the path of life and peace.

6. Matt 3:15.
7. Matt 3:13–17, *NRSV.*
8. John 12:32.
9. John 1:14.
10. John 1:16, *NRSV.*
11. O'Donohue, *Eternal Echoes*, 207.

From this place of surrender to the One who ignited his kingdom life like a burning fire,[12] we might dare to pose one of our most pressing questions: What do we do with our pain? What do we do with our "Martha over-and-against energy," through which we project our residual pain on others?

Jesus responds to such a question by offering his liberating way of journeying through our pain, his freedom-seeking truth that will always take us in the direction of what is most real about our deepest wounding and pain, and his transformative life, which draws us along with the reality of our wounding into greater life: our participation in the internal life of the Trinity.[13] Jesus' restorative way is to transform our wounds into windows, flooding light into the house of our heart, bringing renewal and restoration from the very foundation upwards. Barricaded rooms are gently opened, their hidden fugitives forgiven and welcomed home. Unity is restored and a bright fire burns in its hearth. Little by little, the house of fear is transformed into a house of love and hospitality.

WHOEVER SERVES ME MUST FOLLOW ME: COMPANIONING IN THE WAY OF JESUS

John, the first guide, prepared the way for Jesus, the greater guide, by readily opening a sacred space to receive him and to attend to what he needed most at that particular moment in time—baptism—and so initiates Jesus, the pilgrim, into deeper life, into his true vocation.

12. Matt 3:11, *MSG*.
13. John 8:32; John 14:6.

Through our own transformation, we become witnesses to the freedom and vitality of the new creation that Jesus inaugurated, which furnishes us with hope and vision for a restored humanity. Jesus then invites us to become companions in his way, embodying his life and reflecting his light as we participate more fully in his restorative work. "Whoever serves me must follow me, and where I am, there will my servant be also. Whoever serves me, the Father will honor."[14]

We can learn directly from the "case studies" of the Master Companion about how to value people, how to open safe and restful relational spaces, how to encourage people to be deeply attentive to their experiences, how to work through their resistance to connect them to deeper flows of life-giving love, and how to mend breaches between love and power.

In these personal encounters, whether at a dinner or by a well, Jesus models how to extend his way to pilgrims in the midst of their human experiences, encouraging them towards deeper levels of integrated heart awareness. We may see ourselves in Mary's receptivity or Martha's over-against-ness, and from that place of identification, Jesus offers to draw us, along with our burdens and contradictions, into his gentle and humble heart, that we might receive the greater life running like a living stream beneath the barriers of our life circumstances. As our Mary-like receptivity grows, we become more intimate with this greater guide, who holds grace and truth in perfect unity, freeing us to become more fully human and revealing to us that our true and authentic identity is to be found in God.[15]

14. John 12:26, *NRSV.*
15. John 1:14.

Like John the Baptist, the other companions we are to meet in the following pages encourage pilgrims to journey in the direction of deeper life. But rather than standing in the middle of a river, dressed in camel hair and a leather belt, Andrea (whom we will meet in the next chapter), Amy (whom we will meet in chapters seven and eight), and Stephen (whom we will meet in chapter ten) stand immersed in the streams of human experience. Clothed in Jesus' mantle, they open the way for pilgrims to discover their life in his life of self-giving and other-receiving love and to find enlightenment by his bright burning light. They announce Jesus' coming by helping other pilgrims to be attentive to the movements of grace in the midst of their painful experiences, as well as to the manifestations of his new kingdom life emerging within their own. Daring to leave the safety and security of their therapeutic methods, programs, and strategies for problem-solving, life-management, and recovery on the shore, these guide-companions will plunge into the treacherous rapids of human experience, sustained by the faith that God has placed the firm stepping stones of Jesus' way, truth, and life[16] beneath the water's turbulent surface.

Jesus does not offer us program or method, but invites us to follow him as would-be companions in the way of his death and resurrection, for "unless a grain of wheat falls into the earth and dies, it remains just a single grain; but if it dies, it bears much fruit . . . Those who love their life lose it, and those who hate their life in this world will keep it for eternal life."[17]

16. John 14:6.
17. John 12:24–25, *NRSV*.

3

Following the Golden Thread of Grace

Learn the unforced rhythms of grace.[1]

THE COMPANIONING ROOM

T HIS CHAPTER invites you to become a witness to the encounter between a companion, Andrea Anderson, and a pilgrim, Carol Compton. I imagine myself present to the scene, looking through an observation screen.

As I adjusted my eyes to look through the screen, I saw two women sitting in large and comfortable armchairs. The woman on the left, Andrea,[2] was sitting in a comfortable upright position, hands held loosely in her lap, body slightly forward, indicating a fully awake and attentive posture. Her tender grey eyes did not stare, but rested softly upon the woman opposite, revealing her humble, tender, and compassionate heart. Andrea's gentle demeanour enabled me to

---

1. Matt 11:29, *MSG*.

2. Most of the stories in the book are inspired by a number of individuals rather than being the actual story of one person. This is because personal stories are very sacred and confidential and the identity of pilgrims needs to be protected.

slow my observations and to notice what was happening within myself.

As I lingered with Andrea's heart, I imagined bringing it close to my own, and was rather startled when some of my own wounds and scars began to surface. As this troubling sensation settled, I realized that my inner resonance was connecting with the pain and wounding within Andrea, the companion. Like me, she was a wounded healer.

Andrea's receptivity to the pilgrim displayed a deep sensitivity and vulnerability that was not hidden behind a mask of power or expertise. She did not flinch from pain and was neither afraid nor judgmental about the pilgrim's story. Though she would acknowledge the conflict that is often close to the core of the human soul, Andrea could spaciously and lovingly hold the pilgrim's contradictions and actively encourage her inclination towards goodness—the goodness within her that is of God. Her gentle holding of this pilgrim fully reflected Carl Rogers' three elements of personal congruence, unconditional positive regard, and empathic understanding.[3] Even more than that, she could see beyond the pilgrim's obvious distress and glimpse the inner resourcefulness, beauty, and unique image of God that was at her deepest core. Andrea was bringing the whole of her person, her own contradictions and vulnerability along with her genuine and authentic self—the true part found in God—to place it all in the service of the pilgrim, whom we will call Carol Compton.

I experienced a momentary jolt as I focused on Carol, for she was curled up in obvious pain, her distressed body pressed against the back of the lounge chair, her arms

3. Rogers, *Carl Rogers on Personal Power,* 8–12.

wrapped around a huge cushion, behind which she was hiding her face.

Resisting the urge to become anxious or overwhelmed, I tried to adopt Andrea's calm restfulness and to bring gentleness and humility to my observation. Touched by Carol's heart-felt sobs, I focused my gaze upon her body language and opened my heart to her distress.

Struggling with the urge to comfort Carol and explain what was happening, I noticed that Andrea did not do this and realized that she was not afraid of Carol's pain or visible distress. Little by little, as Carol shared her story, Andrea invited her towards her own safe harbor, where she could bring her story into a place of "rest."

Returning to the beginning, we will now listen to the dialogue between Andrea and Carol. Listening to the dialogue, the invitation is to pay close attention to the relationship forming between companion and pilgrim as Andrea encourages Carol to be attentive to the pain-filled cry emerging from deep within her heart.

THE INVITATION

Giving Carol plenty of time to adjust to the companioning room and settle into her chair, Andrea waited for Carol to look in her direction, indicating without words that she was ready to begin. Then Andrea said, "Carol, I wonder if you could say what it is that you need to attend to in our time together?" Right at the outset, Andrea placed high value on Carol's inner knowing.

"I've been putting-off coming for such a long time," Carol said, explaining that Andrea's phone number had been on a slip of paper stuck in the front of her address book for at least eighteen months. Carol shuddered as she recalled the many times she had reached for the phone, only to pull back at the last minute. Fumbling through her purse, she pulled out the address book and showed Andrea the scrap of paper.

Seeing that Carol was close to tears, Andrea took the slip of paper and holding it back to Carol, gently asked, "What has been so important to you over the last eighteen months that you have kept this number right in the front of your address book?"

"I know that I am going to cry," replied Carol, taking three tissues from the box.

"Just take your time, Carol. You have waited a long time to come to talk about something that is very, very important to you, and now you are here. We don't have to rush."

Like Mary of Bethany having to move beyond cultural, religious, and gender constraints to sit at the feet of Jesus, Carol has had to cross personal, social, and cultural barriers of independence and self-reliance to become vulnerable enough to expose some of her inner darkness to Andrea. The fear is that self-disclosure can lead to rejection, and though Andrea knows this, it is not her task to make a commentary on it. Just as Jesus brings Martha's experience back in front of her for her attention, "Martha, Martha, you are worried and distracted by many things," so Andrea reflects to Carol the feeling beneath her experience: ". . . something that is very, very important to you . . ." Both Jesus and Andrea invite pilgrims to become more attentive to their own experience and to discern what is happening

for them from a level of awareness that is deeper than ordinary, everyday awareness. Both Martha and Carol have a
faculty of soul that, when enlivened, enables them to look
in on, and be prayerfully attentive to, and discerning about
their own experience.

Carol took the slip of paper from Andrea and sat for
a few minutes, examining it before placing it back in her
purse. She then drew her legs up into the ample space of
the lounge chair and covered much of herself with a large
cushion. As her tears began to flow, she moved the cushion
to cover her face, remaining silent and hidden for several
minutes before finally showing her tear-stained face. "It
all seemed to start again when my mother visited just over
eighteen months ago. I had not been in touch with her for at
least two years before that. We don't have good contact. She
will never phone or write to me. I am always reluctant to
get in touch with her because, when I do, it takes me a long
time to get over what seems to happen between us. And I
really wish I knew what does actually happen. I know she
is a very remote sort of person. You would never talk to her
about personal things. I also know she had a terrible time
with my father, who was an alcoholic. She is rather distant
from my children, but that is all right in a way, because I
don't really want them to experience too much of her influence and her negativity."

"I know there is a lot that happened in my childhood,"
she continued, "and that I firmly resolved to be a very different mother to my own children than she was to me. I also
know that it has taken a lot out of me to do that, and a number of times my husband has commented that I just run
myself completely ragged over them. I actually agree with

him. I know that I am doing this, but I simply don't know how to stop it." Carol paused and then repeated, "I don't know how to stop it; I really don't." She paused again and then said more definitely, "And you know, as I talk about it now, I realize that I become even more hyperactive when I have been in contact with my mother."

REFLECTING BACK

Andrea waited for a few moments and then reflected back the last part of what Carol had said: "You find yourself running ragged, even hyperactive I think was the word you used, over your family, you say you don't know how to stop, and that this actually increases when you are in contact with your mother."

"Yes," replied Carol. "That is exactly it."

"I wonder what you are noticing is happening to you right now, Carol, as you hear yourself saying this out loud?"

Carol was silent for a moment and began crying again. "I am feeling incredibly sad, but I am not sure why. But at the same time, I am feeling very angry about this thing that I cannot stop."

"Incredibly sad, but not sure where that is coming from, and angry about this thing that you cannot stop," responded Andrea, pausing when she noticed Carol nodding in reply. "I wonder if you can see this person of yourself: incredibly sad and at the same time angry about what she is finding it difficult to stop."

"Why yes I can," said Carol, as though surprised by this image of herself. "She is right there!"

"As you look at her before you, what do you notice is beginning to happen to her?" inquired Andrea.

"She is not going to allow herself to feel sad," Carol replied.

"She is not going to allow herself to feel sad," echoed Andrea. "When you see that, what do you notice she does next?"

"She just gets frantic and throws herself into activity," said Carol emphatically.

For the next few minutes, with Andrea encouraging her to be attentive to the image right before her, Carol closely observed the person of herself putting all her energy into trying to restore pristine order to a house that was already very clean and tidy. When she had finished, she simply looked for more things to occupy her. It continued non-stop, and Carol said she was starting to feel worn-out just watching all this happening.

"As you now begin to feel worn-out just watching this, what is it that you know is really happening to this woman you are observing?"

"That she is putting all of her energies into avoiding the sadness," she answered, pausing as if looking for more, then added, "and the pain. Yes! She has to avoid both the sadness and the pain." She paused again, and Andrea waited, realizing that Carol was not yet finished. "What was the pain? If I only knew the pain I have put so much into avoiding." Carol looked up at Andrea with her eyes full of tears. "What was the pain I have been frantically running away from for all these years?"

FOLLOWING THE STORY THREAD

At this critical point in the encounter, it is informative to return our gaze to Andrea, who has been closely following the thread of Carol's story.

When I teach, I bring to my classes a ball of wool that has a thin golden twine woven into it. The wool represents the story thread, and as I hold out part of the wool, I encourage participants to always follow the pilgrim's story thread, without introducing anything extraneous to it, placing their trust in the unfolding story. If we are fully and prayerfully attentive to this life as it emerges, we might discern a movement of God's Spirit, a trickle of grace, right in the midst of the pilgrim's experience. This is the golden thread, which you have to look closely to see, or what Eugene Peterson calls, "the unforced rhythms of grace".[4] This golden thread of grace weaves through Carol's life, as it does with other pilgrims, firstly loving her into existence, then loving her redemptively as she grapples with the woundings, the exigencies, and the less than sustaining attachments of her life, and continues to love her towards God's full and final purposes for her.[5] As Andrea brings her full attention to Carol's unfolding story, she is invited to be in relaxed cooperation with these ever present though unforced rhythms of grace.

As Carol's story emerged on the inner screen of her "active imagination," there was an exquisite movement of the Spirit gently coaxing her inner awareness and deeper knowing to the surface, bubbling up like a spring from the inside-out. This mysterious inner figure does not come from an external

4. Matt 11:29, *MSG*.
5. Jinkins, *Invitation to Theology*, 90.

source (such as Andrea, who has stayed faithfully with the task of encouraging Carol to remain attentive to what was emerging in front of her), but from a deep inner longing for freedom and rest—the "Come to me . . ." of Jesus.

ATTENDING TO PAIN

The same gentle Spirit was also moving within Andrea as she opened her humble heart to accompany Carol. Neither Jesus nor Andrea defend their own hearts from the tumult of the pilgrims they are companioning. Just as the heart of Jesus was touched by the deep cry emanating from Martha's fragile heart, Andrea was beginning to notice an intense feeling of pain, like a deep inner cry, steadily pushing its way to the surface, though it did not overwhelm her. As Andrea attended to it, she noticed it held the pain she had experienced of wounding in her relationship with her mother. Because she had very good self-awareness in this area of her life and much healing had occurred, the intense memory of her own painful wounding made her more receptive to the pain that Carol was running away from and sensitized Andrea to its connection with a very deep wounding and trauma. Because this all happened very quickly, it did not impede Andrea's attentiveness to Carol.

Saying nothing about what had happened within herself, Andrea brought her full attention back to Carol and invited her to attend to the pain she'd been avoiding. As Carol stayed with that pain, she said that her inner figure stopped running and turned to explore what she had been fleeing.

As Andrea encouraged Carol to be fully attentive to what was happening for this inner figure, an unseen hand guided Carol to sites of childhood experiences that contained excruciating pain. Along the way, Andrea encouraged Carol's attentiveness by asking questions such as, "What do you notice is happening now?" "What do you notice happens next?" "What is your attention being drawn to?"

Making no external interpretations of the story, Andrea's role remained facilitative as she walked with Carol through her agonizing pain, offering the whole of her authentic and genuine self in the service of Carol.

THE CROSS AS A LISTENING POST

Alongside the ball of wool that I bring to classes, I place a wooden cross from Guatemala, a country that has seen much Christian martyrdom. On the cross is a picture of Jesus, stretched out to embrace the villagers portrayed below. I explain that the cross of Jesus is the best listening post under which to receive, in our embrace, stories of pain and suffering. It is the Christ who is needed in the midst of such experiences, for he invites pilgrims to let go of the pain and suffering that has entangled and imprisoned them for so long. Because this letting go can feel like dying, the invitation needs to be accompanied by a life-giving and forgiving love that is stronger than the fear that has protectively bound the pilgrim or (as in Carol's case) kept her running. As we bring our gaze to the cross, we remember that, in the presence of this powerful love, "rising" can follow such "dying". A faith-committed companion like Andrea, who reflected the companioning way of Jesus throughout her entire encounter with Carol, quietly moved into the back-

ground and became witness to these sacred and life transforming moments.

If our task is to reflect and embody the icon of human restoration and freedom that is the person of Jesus,
this icon holds within it a cross, a place of both death and
resurrection.

ENCOUNTERING THE WOUNDED CHILD

What follows is a brief review of one of the major threads
in Carol's unfolding story. The figure of herself that Carol
had been observing on her inner screen took her to a place
in her childhood, where she was used as an intermediary
between her mother and an alcoholic and violent father. By
observing the child persona of her inner figure very carefully, the adult Carol re-entered and re-experienced critical
childhood events—almost like watching a video, yet very
real. This latent capacity (identified as our "active imagination") enables us to access deeper realms of our lived experience. Most need a companion to remain focussed, trustful
of what is emerging and safe for such an inner journey.

In this way, Carol re-engaged with the long-forgotten
memories and traumas she experienced as a child; she had
hidden them away. Without a sympathetic adult witness,
Carol had been left alone with traumas far too overwhelming for a young child to hold, and so she had resolved to
get away from an intolerable family situation at the earliest
opportunity. As she engaged with these hidden memories,
a question emerged for Carol, a painful puzzle she longed
to solve: Why had her mother not protected her? Why had
she been used in this way?

Wrestling with these questions, Carol heard the pain-filled cry of an unwanted child who had never had the opportunity to bond with her own mother. For many minutes, Carol sobbed heart-breaking lamentations. In the midst of this devastation, Jesus manifested himself to Carol. Up until this time, Andrea had reflected something of Jesus' way to Carol, so when His manifest presence appeared, it was almost as an extension of Andrea. But slowly, Jesus revealed to Carol, in a unique way, that her truest and most trustworthy parent was indeed her Heavenly Father. During this moment, Andrea moved back a little, while encouraging the adult Carol to be attentive to what was unfolding in front of her.

TRANSFORMING PAIN

How were Carol and Andrea able to continue on in spite of the overwhelming pain? First, Andrea guided Carol to ensure that she remained in the transcendent adult-observer role as the images of this traumatized and unwanted child emerged before her. An adult is able to carry much more than a child and has more capacity to digest such events and then evacuate the afflictive emotions that have been stored-up around these wounds. Second, Andrea knew that the painful stories and afflictive emotions that for so long had been trying to push their way upwards into Carol's conscious adult awareness were vital for her restoration as an adult woman, a mother, a wife, a daughter, and a friend.

Carol's running had become untenable and unsustainable. To alter course she needed to turn around and engage the pain and fear that had so entrapped her. Part of Carol needed to die so that she could live more abundantly and find deep rest for her soul.

Andrea did not fuss over Carol or use words of consolation or comfort when she discovered that her mother had never wanted her. Instead, she kept Carol attentive to what was emerging in front of her so that she wouldn't run from the overwhelming pain of rejection. Right in the midst of Carol's devastating discovery, Andrea asked: "What do you notice is now happening to you as you discover that you were not wanted by your mother?"

This is a question that can break a companion's heart to ask, yet Andrea held the hope of a restored reality that was even deeper than Carol's pain. It was to hold hope in the face of despair. To ask this question, she had to know that resurrection can follow death and that painful self-knowledge goes hand in hand with a deeper knowledge of God.[6] It was Andrea's hope in the resurrection that stretched the horizon of her vision far beyond what she ordinarily would have thought to be possible. Though the mind will find such knowing almost impossible to grasp, the soul can weep for the paradise Carol lost, while at the same time receiving the embrace of the One in whom it is being restored. As a companion in the way of Jesus, Andrea's faith was continually challenging her to reshape her understanding and opening her to possibilities that were genuinely new.[7]

When Andrea asked Carol about being an unwanted child, it brought both pilgrim and companion to the door, where Jesus was waiting, lamp in hand. As Carol stepped across this threshold with Jesus, a significant part of herself

6. Green, *Opening to God,* 81.
7. Jinkins, *Invitation to Theology,* 30.

died with him. Yet because Andrea, who had herself felt the pain of Carol's dying, knew that he was "the resurrection and the life,"[8] she could trust that Carol would rise into a new, restored, and more abundant life. Carol's most painful place of wounding became the location of Jesus' deepest healing and transformation. Her soul reconnected with her true life source, and the wound of her "unwantedness" became a window to her eternal belonging. There was no more need to run!

IN THE COMPANIONING ROOM

Returning to the observation room to look in on the encounter between Andrea and Carol, I could see that the room appeared to be gilded in gold, with pearl inlay, the figures backlit by a blue moony light,[9] reminding me that the soul, in all of its shyness, will only reveal itself to gentle attentiveness, watching, and praying. The soul does not yield to direct observation or cognitive analysis. Having learned to value the way the soul will offer up its story thread and how it can do this in cooperation with the inner movements of grace, Andrea's simple questions encouraged Carol to be attentive to her inner life as it emerged before her.

8. John 11:25, *NRSV.*

9. Adapted from William Blake's poem, "The Crystal Cabinet." In Sampson, *The Poems,* 206–7.

4

Treading the Air of Mystery

I came that they may have life,
and have it abundantly.[1]

BEYOND OUR LITTLENESS

W HEN AWAY from the interface of city lights, it is a
gift to lie back and gaze at the stars. Recently, while
in that reclining posture, a friend said, "Imagine you were
looking down upon the stars rather than looking up at them.
You might get the feeling of falling off the earth." As I sought
to adjust my gaze I entertained two opposing thoughts: I
could free-fall into the vortex of this immensity to my certain destruction, or I could grow wings, learn to tread the
air and embark on a great voyage of discovery. How quickly
my imagination was sparked by such oblique viewing! How
sobering the close proximity between my thoughts towards
self-discovery and self-destruction.[2] While there is but
one soul, its faculties and energies can be gathered up and

---

1. John 10:10, *NRSV.*

2. "Can two opposing souls be found within one breast?" Wolfgang
von Goethe, *Goethe's Faust,* 145.

drawn in opposing directions, thus we need some force, like gravity, to keep us safe and grounded.

In this chapter we enter the world of oblique viewing, where the companion trusts what God reveals through faithful and prayerful attentiveness. As a companion, I need to expand the eyes and ears of my heart each day in order to enter the mystery of oblique viewing; otherwise I will only see and hear what fits with my logic concerning people's psychological functioning. But by gazing more obliquely, I might grow new wings and "by indirections find directions out,"[3] thus learning to tread the air of mystery that surrounds the inner vastness of the human soul.

When we stand in the presence of something greater than ourselves, the faculties of the soul are enlivened and we are filled with awe and wonderment. My stargazing reminded me of my smallness and the frailness of my heartbeat should I ever try to pit it against the power of the heart that energizes and holds the entire cosmos in harmony. Yet I do this whenever I adopt an over-against-stance to my life. Though I desire to have the Mary of Bethany heart of receptivity, I often find myself reacting more like Martha, trying to inflate my smallness to battle life circumstances, allowing my ego perceptions to reign in my little kingdom. It can seem more manageable to pretend the cosmic heart is too distant, across too wide a chasm that no free-fall nor flight could ever span.

Purposeful engagement with our deeper life-giving energies will enable us to bring more of our whole person to our active engagement in our world, helping us make the shift from reacting over-and-against our life circumstances

3. Shakespeare, *Hamlet,* Act 2, Scene 1, line 66.

to proactively responding to life and what it asks of us. The journey of self-discovery and of soul-awakening is never an end in itself, but its purpose is to tap into our true vitality, deeper knowing, imagination, sharpened senses, courage, emotional resourcefulness, creativity, even our wound-edness and pain in order to liberate these faculties from self-serving motives and our propensity towards self-de-struction. We need to submit them to the guidance of God's Spirit and offer each for the service of God's kingdom.

Yet Jesus, who incarnates the cosmic heart of God and also forms a bridge across it,[4] reaches out to me, and em-braces my fragile heart in the flow of His Father's abiding love.[5] God has gifted my vulnerable person with life-giving faculties of hearing, seeing, perceiving, along with a desire for intimacy with Him and a longing to extend His flow of love to others.[6]

Memory can also bring to mind the visual beauty of a flower, the songs of birds, the taste of the eucalyptus leaf, the smells of the forest, and the caress of the morning breeze upon my cheek. Each of these senses adds its unique texture to my visual remembrances. The physicality of my body can recall aching limbs and shortness of breath from steep climbs. The chambers of my imagination can hold a foretaste of communion with nature well before my body arrives on site. Spiritual sensibilities can lift my gaze above this vivid recall of beautiful scenery and offer gratitude and praise to its Creator. I do honor to these experiences when I hold my attentiveness long enough to reengage with

4. John 1:18.
5. John 15:16.
6. Deut 11:13; 13:3; Josh 22:5; Matt 22:37–39.

their richness and allow myself, all over again, to be taken by their surprises. Recollection can be an ongoing part of the experience, a way of deepening and giving meaning to it as well as adding to its enjoyment. My memory archive can be prompted by a photograph, a conversation about our travels, a familiar smell, a wistful longing to return, or the sorrow I felt when I stepped across a dead possum.

But these faculties can atrophy through neglect and even become shadows of themselves, leading to my destruction.[7] My heart, with its potential to bring together all of these endowments of consciousness in the service of my Creator, becomes hardened and siphoned-off in the service of many gods of my own making—gods with contemporary titles, such as, "realizing my dreams," "finding myself," "self-expression," and "personal fulfillment."[8]

When turning our gaze towards the immense vastness of our inner landscape, we can engage our thoughts, feelings, imagination, spiritual sensibilities, senses, longings, and desires, meaning making, awe, wonder, body sensations, and much more, yet this landscape often remains foreign, even alien, and foreboding. So if we have these vital energies of the soul, why do we remain relative strangers to our inner landscape? What entraps us at the surface levels of our experiences and confines us to the very small rim of our existence?

7. Jer 5:21; Mark 8:17–18.
8. Green, *Opening to God,* 29.

MARTHA'S LIFE ON THE RIM

While the image of Mary's receptivity and openness as she sat in the presence of Jesus is inviting, it is also unsettling. After all, someone has to get the job done! Somebody has to take charge! When we jump to Martha's defense, we fail to see how opportunistic the ego is in taking our reins, and so we may not notice it limiting and constraining us to live on the small rim it chooses for our existence. Annie Dillard helps to unmask something of the littleness of our Martha-like energy.[9] "There is always an enormous temptation," she suggests, "in all of life to diddle around making itsy-bitsy friends and meals and journeys for itsy-bitsy years on end." She then offers a rather stinging critique and suggests that, what we have been referring to here as our "rim-like existence" is actually to stand over-and-against the gift of grace—the same gift of grace that brings us into relationship with the great heart that gives us life. Of this small life she says, "It is so self-conscious, so apparently moral, simply to step aside from the gaps where the creeks and winds pour down, saying, I never merited this grace, quite rightly, and then to sulk along the rest of your days on the edge of rage."

It can be hard to acknowledge that in our chosen "littleness," our soul faculties might wither and our soul energies might be captured by a negativity that simmers just below the surface. There is a life breath, a source of vitality, a knowing, an imagining, a thirsting, and a longing harbored deep within each of us, but there is also impoverishment when we remain strangers to the life force that uniquely shapes who we are. What is most at stake are the parts that

9. Dillard, *Pilgrim at Tinker Creek,* 274.

self-discovery and the awakening of our soul play for all of us in stepping up into the fullness of who we are—beings created to be in communion with, and to reflect the likeness of our Creator.

In our impoverishment we seek external markers for our identity, adorning our bodies with designer clothes while accepting rags for our inner decorations, coveting jewelry from far-off places while remaining oblivious to gems that already glisten within, purchasing bunches of flowers from the local florist while those in our inner gardens blush unseen.

Yet, as Martha's story unfolds following her transforming encounter with Jesus, we do see her choosing to receive relationship with One far greater, wiser, wilder, and more extravagant in love than herself—One who would soon resurrect her brother, Lazarus—and to grow into this wisdom, wildness, and extravagance of love.

RESURRECTING THE INNER LIFE

The fact that Mary and Martha later witnessed the resurrection of their brother, Lazarus, should not be lost on us.[10] For Mary, and later for Martha, there was a resurrection to greater inner life, which significantly impacted her outer life. Mary of Bethany is a beautiful and life-giving sign for us, as her life can guide us to a deep inner place of sitting with a heart fully open to the presence of Jesus.

We meet Mary in the beginning of her openness and receptivity, and we journey with her into the deeper places of her heart awareness, where she comes in touch with the one

10. John 11.

thing that is needed. Then we witness her moving right into the fullness and extravagance of her personhood as she takes expensive perfume and anoints Jesus' feet,[11] rising to her peak moment in human history. If we gaze upon her obliquely, she reveals some of the mysteries of the human soul.

As Mary sits at the feet of the One who incarnates for her the great, three-person heart, her fragile heart is embraced in the same flow of life-giving and soul-enhancing love that moves freely between its own members.[12] This comes to her as gift, grace. As she welcomes this gift, it begins to mirror something of its essence and consciousness within her heart.

There is the outer scene of hospitality, with some of its strains and stresses, going on around her. There is an inner table where the guests of Mind, Intuition, Relational Knowing, Body Awareness, and Spiritual Sensitivity have all gathered to share a meal. Words of thanksgiving are spoken with the presence of Jesus acknowledged by all assembled. A spacious sense of oneness and of unity begins to emerge. The energies and the desires of Mary's soul are stirred and drawn from their slumber, shy of some of these guests, especially when they meet them alone. One by one they show their face and begin to serve the guests and to wait graciously upon the One they know, when fully awake and attentive, as their Lord. It is in his presence that these guests, and the energies and desires of Mary's soul which serve them, realize they are all significant parts of her; they are all one.

Reignited and raised in the service of greater life, these faculties, energies, and deep desires are gathered together

11. John 12:3.
12. John 15:16.

by the golden cord of their Lord's Spirit, drawn into deep intimacy with him as they begin to participate more fully in his life, extending his flow of love to others.[13]

Martha, on the other hand, is still captive by a shadow lord who has tried to establish a safe and secure refuge, but has actually created a prison. This shadow lord co-opts the self-protective energies of Martha's ego and offers in exchange a persona of hospitality, along with the belief that she is in control. A tenuous veil of protection is draped over this tiny realm, bringing uniformity of color, a judicial function of appropriating blame on outsiders, and a power mechanism that negates the influences and incursions of others. The faculties, energies, and desires of soul that are more shy, struggle to find a place here, but the more brazen of their shadow brothers and sisters manage quite well.

There are many tiny fractures in Martha's brittle, protective covering, along with a niggling sense of not keeping faith with a deeper truth. Jesus' presence will be destabilizing for her as the shy and slumbering soul community are inwardly stirred by his gentle and humble heart, and drawn back into their purpose by his inviting Spirit. Martha demonstrates the workings of grace in and around our fragile lines of resistance.

COMPANIONING: THE JOURNEY INWARDS

In the previous chapter, Carol found the vantage point of attentiveness by shifting her perspective and entering her active imagination. This enabled her to re-experience child-

13. Deut 11:13; 13:3; Josh 22:5; Matt 22:37–39.

hood memories, crossing a threshold from ordinary awareness into deeper awareness.

Carol needed a guide to lead her across this threshold so that she would have the courage to bypass the sentries she had placed on guard so many years before. Up to this point she had believed that what was on the other side was dark, shameful, sad, brimming over with pain and fear. Painful as it was, she began to engage with the buried half of her life, where she experienced a transforming touch and moved forward with a greater sense of wholeness, realizing it would be an ongoing journey.

In the last chapter, what blocked Carol from knowing the pain that she had put so much energy into avoiding? Carol's story had always been with her, and many times she had sought resolution, but something stood in her way. Prior to the session with Andrea, Carol had been frantically scrambling up a high mountain in search of a vantage point from which to view and make sense of her own landscape. However, when she reached observation platforms along the way, the view was obscured by a thick blanket of fog. It is significant that she'd had Andrea's contact details in her purse for eighteen months before making this appointment. Each time she took it out of her purse, longing to enter more deeply into her inner world, something had caused her to draw back.

Eventually, the journey up the mountain brought her to the platform, upon which she met Andrea, her guide. The relational space Andrea opened and the gentle responses and questions that invited Carol to attend to her experiences enabled Carol, little-by-little, to turn around to catch the edges of a panoramic view from the other side of the platform. As Andrea sought to reflect the way of Jesus, who offers sight to the blind and light to those who walk in darkness, she invited Carol to radically shift her perspective.[14] This does not mean that Andrea saw clearly everything that was happening to Carol, or that she knew Carol's story better than Carol knew it herself. But this different way of being in the world gave Andrea enough faith to stand in the fog with Carol, holding the hope that Carol would find her inner sight and receive the one true Guide, who could bring life and enlightenment to her fog-bound world.

14. John 8:12.

5

Drawing Near the Well

A woman, a Samaritan, came to draw water.
Jesus said, "Would you give me a drink?"[1]

THE SAMARITAN WOMAN
ENCOUNTERS JESUS

To find our way into the deeper, interior reaches of the story of the woman at the well, below the surface-level responses of the Samaritan woman, we will need to make our viewing position oblique, as we did in the last chapter, by bringing our hearts close to this woman's heart and to the loving heart of our Master guide. An oblique view of this encounter enables us to enter with our imagination the different parts of the woman's inner being.

Written imaginatively, this reflection is offered as a celebration of how the faculties and energies of our souls can be enlivened and restored, and our sacred places indwelt as we enter, little by little, into intimate and restorative relationship with the living Word. The way of Jesus reflects a profound relational transformation which works its way

1. John 4:7, *MSG.*

outwards from our inmost parts as, through his spirit, his life is engendered within us. He stretches the horizon of our vision beyond all that we might dream or imagine.[2] As his kingdom breaks into our lives, and into the world immediately around us, we join him in singing the songs of Zion in lands which have become increasing estranged from their sounds. As companions in his way we momentarily lay down the residues of our psychological paradigms and listen for the faint echoes of these songs as they rise up from the depths of the human soul.[3] And as we enter our imagination there is even room for a little playfulness!

RESTING AT THE WELL

Coming upon a man resting by the well from which she needed to draw water, the woman flung a protective veil around herself to create as much distance as possible. He was obviously Jewish and could treat her like a dog. When he condescended to speak to her, she was caught completely unaware.

"Would you give me a drink of water?"[4]

That he asked something of her rang warning bells. Men always had mixed motives! She should rise up, put all the religious, cultural, and gender barriers back in his face, and never let him know he had the upper hand!

And yet, was something beginning to stir within her? Can we bring our imagination to this place?

2. Jinkins, *Invitation to Theology*, 30.
3. Ps 137: 1–4.
4. John 4:7 *MSG*.

Indeed, a tiny golden beam of warm light gently touched upon Longing's face, causing her to shelter her eyes and rub sleep from them. "A thirsty traveler asking the woman for a drink—unusual," she mused. "But that voice is strangely familiar," she continued, rolling over in her bed. But the echo of this voice continued to bounce on the back of her mind, as if to stir a fuddled memory. Longing rose from her bed and went in search of Recollection, whom she found to be in a deep sleep. She was reluctant to wake her, as she knew how exhausted Recollection was from her endless daily toil.

Recollection's nickname was Spider, for each day she would spin a web of fine gossamer thread around the regions of the woman's heart to catch all the fragments of her experience in the hope that they might become useful for her attentiveness and prayer. She would faithfully store them in a golden room, similar to the one the observer had witnessed in Carol's story in chapter three, with its inlaid pearl and its crystal bright. With the passing of time many of the fragments would entangle and rip her precious web. Recollection would have to ask Mercy to help stretcher away the residue into Soul's Infirmary, where it was becoming increasingly difficult to find spare life-support equipment, as most of it was in constant use. Finally, Recollection woke and joined Longing, and they strained to recognize the voice of the thirsty traveler.

Then Truth Pilgrim arrived, out of breath, with earth from the garden and the sweat of toil upon her forehead. She would rise early most mornings to tend the soil around the small plants of deeper truth in a garden that, nowadays, hardly anyone visited. Leaning on her garden fork as she tried to catch her breath, she panted, "It is His voice; I have heard His voice. It is the voice of the Lord who speaks over the waters".[5] And as they all now listened intently, it was not only his voice they where noticing, but also the rhythmic beating of a gentle and humble heart. There was also something in his spirit that was drawing them. They were joined by Deep Desire, who herself was constantly thirsty, and whose curiosity had been heightened by the request for a drink and by the thirsty voice.

"It seems so long ago," sighed Recollection, whose mind had been very busy since she was awakened. "It is like the voice of the One who was with us at the woman's birth." There was a long pause. "Yes, indeed," exclaimed Recollection. It is the voice of the One who first gave us breath. Longing and Deep Desire needed no more convincing. They were about to hurry off to rouse the others when they stopped in their tracks.

"If you knew the gift of God, and who it is that is saying to you, 'Give me a drink,' you would have asked him, and he would have given you living water."[6]

Deep Desire gasped in disbelief. So often she had felt diminished from the pain of waiting. The thirst was so great. She knew that her weeping would endure for a night, but her vigil had been long and the night never-ending. Was this to be the morning of her joy?[7] Her whole being now strained to hear and receive everything he said, and each word he spoke carried with it a huge droplet of water that splashed upon her parched tongue.

5. John 10:27; 18:37; Ps 29:3.

6. John 4:10, *NRSV*.

7. Ps 30:5.

Recollection exclaimed to Longing, "He is speaking in our language!"

Longing replied, "I so wish Imagination was here because she would help us see more of what he is offering." For a moment their thoughts turned to Imagination, who had become rather lost of late and their concern was that she was spending far too much time with Fantasy and Daydream. Both seemed to have distracted Imagination from her chores, as this trio would wander off to play. In better days, Imagination could sit quietly in the presence of mystery and bring the others closer to what was being revealed through her images, metaphors, and simple parables. In her company these would become more real than real and would touch something deep throughout the soul community. "She could certainly help us now." Longing sighed and shifted her gaze from the thirsty traveler to the water jar, then back to the well as she pondered the inviting words, "living water."

All were delighted when Imagination suddenly appeared, having heard such kind mention of her name. She had left Fantasy and Daydream to continue with their game.

"Everyone who drinks of this water will be thirsty again, but those who drink of the water that I will give them will never be thirsty. The water that I will give will become in them a spring of water gushing up to eternal life."[8]

Deep Desire and Longing first noticed the trickle of water and followed it to its source, where they found that a small spring had begun to bubble up in their midst. Recollection found Mercy and both hurried to the partially

8. John 4:13–14, *NRSV.*

darkened ward of the infirmary, where Feeling, Emotion, and Passion had long lain almost completely immobilized, constrained by a serious illness that Balm had diagnosed as the virus, "numbness." Not only had it been a life-threatening disease for this trio, but it had given free-range to the errant attributes of some of their siblings, including Anger, who was now being referred to as Rage. Sorrow, who had been such a valued companion, had fled into hiding, almost as if for her life. It was difficult for the others, for she had taken with her the key to the blue back-lit chamber that held Great Sadness.

"Numbness" was a very contagious virus, and many of the important functions of the soul community were now being carried out in a rather perfunctory manner. On entering the ward, Mercy drew back the drapes and a beam of golden light fell across the beds that contained the three almost motionless forms of Feeling, Emotion, and Passion. Even before Longing arrived in the room with a large jug that had been filled from a new spring, a tiny teardrop had formed in the corner of Feeling's eye.

"Go, call your husband, and come back…You are right in saying, 'I have no husband;' for you have had five husbands, and the one you have now is not your husband. What you have said is true!"[9]

One member of the community, Lady Poverty of Spirit, was grounded in the reality of the woman's life, but had lost her voice when another of the more errant members, Denial, had gained hers. For truth to be finally spoken was music to her ears, and for truth to be acknowledged by the One who held both grace and truth in perfect unity in

9. John 4:16–18, *NRSV.*

his person and presence, was joy to her heart. Lady Poverty intuitively knew that the journey towards wholeness, not only for the woman, but also for the soul community, had to move in the direction of what was most real. "Finally," she mused to herself, "there is One who can lead us back into our lived experience." To name what is true, however dark and shameful, in the presence of this One who is both life and light, is to drink from this inner spring of water and to be bathed in his forgiving love.

The mantra that Lady Poverty had for so long carried in her heart could now be spoken out loud: "Blessed are the poor in spirit, for theirs is the kingdom of heaven." [10]

No sooner had these words passed her lips than a kindred response came, almost as an echo: "Blessed are those who mourn, for they will be comforted." To her delight, they were spoken by her sister, Sorrow, who had just returned from her self-imposed exile.

"Woman, believe me, the hour is coming when you will worship the Father neither on this mountain nor in Jerusalem. You worship what you do not know; we worship what we know, for salvation is from the Jews."[11]

The words, "the hour is coming," touched the emptiness deep in Recollection, as it did in Longing and Deep Desire. Could this be what they had been looking for? Could this be their time at long last?

Recollection sought out Archivist, and both rummaged in the deepest recesses of soul's archives for an ancient text in the hope that it would reveal something of this new hour. As they carried it out and laid it before the

10. Matt 5:3, *NRSV.*
11. John 4:21–22, *NRSV.*

others, their whole story emerged. The re-telling of it was music to their ears and honey to their mouths: the story of their creation, their garden, God's covenant with them, His promises to them, opening out before them as the scroll was unfurled, and fluttering about in the breeze. "Why is it," some exclaimed in amazement, "that we have only been fed on small tattered fragments for so long?"

"...the hour is coming, and is now here, when the true worshipers will worship the Father in spirit and truth, for the Father seeks such as these to worship him. God is spirit, and those who worship him must worship in spirit and truth."[12]

The whole community leapt up and began a spring cleaning. The air was charged with anticipation as they worked together. Doors that had been closed for years were sprung open, their moldy contents sorted—some for the garage sale, some for the bonfire. And there was still much work that would be needed in the future. Musky drapes were washed, repaired, and rehung so that the warm, golden light could penetrate every nook and cranny. A new day was dawning and all was fresh and bright. Soon everything was in readiness. Only one question remained: Would the woman recognize the thirsty traveler and invite him in?

The garden at the entrance to his dwelling had been carefully and lovingly tended, and there was no trace of the vines that had long tangled around and obscured its portal. The intricately carved and inlaid lintel and doorway had been so highly polished that all could see their reflections. As the work of each was completed, they gathered there with hearts full of hope, that this indeed might be the day.

12. John 4:23–24, *NRSV*.

No one had ever seen inside this dwelling, as he alone had its only key. Some said the same key could re-open Eden's gates, while others suggested the seeds of the tree of life itself were held in trust behind this door. One soul sage said that this dwelling contained a reflection of the glory of God and that His name was etched on every facet of a diamond so pure that it could reflect the dazzling light of heaven. This was held safe from any taint of the woman's sin or illusion, as a sacred deed of inheritance, designating her as daughter, should she choose to acknowledge His name.[13]

"I am he, the one who is speaking to you."[14] "You don't have to wait any longer or look any further."[15]

The anticipation amongst the assembled throng rose as the woman spoke of the Messiah. Longing knew that the woman had for many years hoped that someone would come and save her from her oppressive circumstances. Daydream and Fantasy left their game of imagining a great warrior, who would come to take the woman to live in a palace, to see what was happening. Lady Poverty's spirits had been lifted by the woman's earlier acknowledgement of her true circumstances, and she could see that she was on the very edge of newness, healing, and transformation. Feeling, Emotion, and Passion were all standing on tiptoe in a state of readiness, knowing they might be needed at any moment. Senses' family of five, who had rarely communicated over the last few years, were all holding hands, with

13. Influenced by Thomas Merton in McDonnell, *A Merton Reader*, 347.

14. John 4:26, *NRSV*.

15. John 4:26, *MSG*.

their precious faculties finely attuned. All held their breath as the woman now hurried back to her village.

A great cheer went up as the woman ran amongst the people of her village, informing them of the traveler and what had happened. "Could this be the Messiah?" she called out to them. But within, there was a knowing and a rejoicing. "This is indeed the One!"

With this acknowledgement, Praise stepped forward to lead the congregation in a hymn of thanksgiving.[16] "Long my imprisoned spirit lay," they sang, "fast-bound in sin and nature's night," giving expression to what they had lived through. "Thine eye diffused a quickening ray; I woke—the dungeon flamed with light!" The warm golden light that had penetrated each nook and cranny now flooded around them. "My chains fell off, my heart was free!" Every eye flooded with tears and every heart filled to the brim with thanksgiving for their new freedom. "I rose, went forth, and followed Thee!" Their liberator had finally come. He was indeed the glory, the joy, and the crown of this woman's soul. Awe and Wonder in unison repeated the word, "glory." Gratitude's benediction gave voice to what was on every heart as she cried:

> We stretch out our hands to you;
> It is for You our soul has thirsted,
> Like a parched and barren land.[17]

A rebirth had occurred in the community of soul. Members who had taken much power over the community,

16. Charles Wesley, *Amazing Love (And can it be), The Methodist Hymn Book*, 329.

17. Adapted from Ps 143:6.

such as Fear, Pride, Envy, Enmity, Lethargy, and Indolence, had all shrunk in stature, some returning to their outlying caves with heads hung low. It was amazing to see Worry and High Alert more relaxed. There were tears in the eyes of those who saw them coming in from the fields, carrying great bunches of lilies to decorate the once neglected assembly hall. There had been much activity in refurbishing this great room, which had been re-named the "Great Hall of Heart". The broken dining tables and chairs had been repaired and polished. A horseshoe shape of easy chairs had been placed around the hearth, and the fireplace was tended constantly. All the lamps around the walls had been lit from the golden beams of Jesus' light. A great feast was being organized in his honor. The simple plan for the evening was that following the meal, all would sit around the fire to ponder how to continue to nurture the soul community in its collective desire to offer adoration and service to this guest and to establish a firm foundation of peace and rest for the woman's soul.

Their guest gave them each an exquisite cord of fine gold and showed them how to weave all of the pieces into one spirit, one accord. During the weaving, each asked forgiveness of the other. Complete unity and renewal had not yet been achieved, for that would be an ongoing task, but it would be brought to fulfillment at a subsequent visit, the timing of which was not for them to know.[18] He then drew them into deeper intimacy as he broke the bread of his own body and offered the wine of his own blood, inviting them to continue this memorial feast in remembrance of him.[19]

18. Matt 24:44.
19. Luke 22:19–20.

One of the matters raised at a subsequent meeting was how to assist the woman, and those like her, to find greater intimacy with their inner landscape. Ego was clearly outvoted on her call for deep introspection and the development of what she labeled, "a scrupulous conscience." Instead, the community wanted to nurture self-wakefulness in the woman, that she might grow in the knowledge and love of the living God.

COMPANIONING IN THE WAY OF JESUS: A DANCE WITH RESISTANCE

Returning to the beginning of this account of the Samaritan woman by gazing through the companioning window, we see that she is almost completely closed, heavily protected, and exerting great energy to hold together the basic residue of her integrity. Her stance is almost completely self-protective and defensive.

We also notice how constrained and entangled she is, living on the restrictive rim of her existence. Through her wounding and choices, her living space has contracted; her life-giving soul faculties are experiencing neglect; she has become alienated from many people in her community and also from her inner-self. Yet if we move our position closer to the gentle and humble heart of Jesus, our guide, we encounter her wounded and fragile heart. Beneath the many layers of protection is a cry for someone to come alongside to save her from her oppressive circumstances, to save her from herself.

Patiently and gently, Jesus loves his way through the many external and internal barriers that for so long have bound and entangled this woman's heart, cooperating with the unforced movements of grace that loosen the soil at the base of these barriers.[20] As their eyes meet, she thirsts for One whom she had hardly dared to believe would come.

The trickles of grace gently penetrate the cracks that open up in her thin protective covering and become a tiny spring deep down inside her, washing over her and transforming the wounded parts of her inner being. Jesus does not fight her resistance, but lovingly dances with it, drawing the woman to the site of her wounding, her place of pain. "Go, call your husband, and come back."[21]

This could seem a jolt in the conversation, until we notice that Jesus holds this place of wounding, pain, and shame tenderly, within cupped hands: one hand is grace, the other is truth. Able to hold her contradictions, along with the frayed and fragmented parts of her person, in his unified self, he asks her to be truthful until the point of healing is reached.

Though the woman still stands by the well, she is drawn deeper towards her inner well, one that has long held the life-giving faculties, energies, and desires of her soul, all of which have been named and evoked within her by the thirsty traveler. We witness her soul coming to life as she exclaims to others: "Come, see a man who knew all about the things I did, who knows me inside and out. Do you think this could be the Messiah?"[22]

This story reveals to us, as companions, Jesus' profound and masterful way of engaging with resistance in

20. "Learn the unforced rhythms of grace." Matt 11:29, *MSG*.

21. John 4:16, *NRSV*.

22. John 4:29, *MSG*.

order to evoke and enliven greater life. There is no clash, nor is there any sign of defensiveness in him, even when the woman is defensive and rude. Instead, there is spaciousness and a capacity to discern a heavily muffled heart cry. This encounter offers a wonderful expression of how our soul life can be raised up and re-ignited as we come into communion with the greater life and light of Jesus. With the golden cord of his spirit, Jesus can reach to the depths of our being, gather together our dissipated and frayed faculties, energies, and desires, and draw us towards a life of adoration and service—a life in which we move in the direction of wholeness and holiness to become more truly and fully who we were created to be.[23]

23. John 4:24.

6

Enlivening the Senses, Waking the Heart

Blessed are your eyes, for they see,
and your ears, for they hear.[1]

JESUS COMPANIONS THE RELIGIOUS LAWYER

WHEN A religious lawyer comes to test Jesus by asking, "What must I do to inherit eternal life?"[2] he draws the man back into his area of knowing: "What is written in the law? What do you read there?" The lawyer responds: "You shall love the Lord your God with all your heart, and with all your soul, and with all your strength, and with all your mind; and your neighbor as yourself." All the lawyer needs is contained in this wonderful expression of a full and wholly integrated consciousness, yet his predisposition towards religious legalism reveals that it is a response of his mind rather than of his heart and soul. Though the lawyer gives the right answer, Jesus knows that the deeper law has not yet spilled over into the way the lawyer treats his neigh-

---

1. Matt 13:16, *NRSV.*
2. Luke 10:25–37, *NRSV.*

bor. So Jesus replies: "You have given the right answer; do this, and you will live".

"And who is my neighbor?" the lawyer asks, as if to justify himself. Slipping between the sentries of legal certainty that are strongly guarding the lawyer's heart, Jesus offers him the parable of the Good Samaritan, a story brimming over with imagery and metaphor, with actions of compassion and mercy. This parable holds the capacity to destabilize the lawyer's certitudes and re-ignite his stunted soul life, reflecting the gentle and humble heart of the storyteller, along with his restorative purposes.

Through this parable, Jesus, the storyteller, draws the lawyer into a story, rather than a debate about law. The plot is familiar: a good man is beaten-up, robbed, and left for dead. The characters are familiar, too: a priest and a Levite, important and busy men with important things demanding their attention. Though the lawyer may feel some discomfort when they don't intervene, since he has just spoken words about loving your neighbor as yourself, he identifies with the priest and the Levite, making his judgment ambivalent and uncertain.

The next character, the Samaritan, is totally alien, and so it is easy for the lawyer to distance himself, even though the alien is doing what the lawyer senses he should be doing. The innkeeper may be a little more familiar, but the abundant generosity and care shown by the Samaritan challenges the lawyer, because the Samaritan's actions are so foreign to the lawyer's experience. This alien character in a parable often represents something within the listener that has become repressed. In this parable, excessive preoccupation with religious legalism has repressed mercy within the lawyer. As the storyteller, Jesus, invites the lawyer to recover the deeper, un-lived Good Samaritan aspect of his interior life, which is less confined and restricted than his surface life of religious legalism and certainty, devoid of love, grace, mercy, and truth. By engaging the lawyer in a deeper level of awareness, the parable prepares him to receive Jesus' question: "Which of these three, do you think, was a neighbor to the man who fell into the hands of the robbers?" The lawyer, far more receptive now, responds, "The one who showed him mercy". Jesus can now say, to one who now has ears to hear, "Go and do likewise."

Jesus guides the lawyer by way of his heart, the centre of his consciousness, where the faculties of the soul can love "the Lord your God with all your heart, and with all your soul, and with all your strength, and with all your mind; and your neighbor as yourself." By intimately participating in God's purposes for our lives and the world, we find peace, balance, a complete identity, and rest.

If the lawyer can "live into" this commandment, he will not have to defend himself with self-protective argument or legalese.[3] His intuition, feelings, emotions, and passions will heighten his awareness; his imagination will bring him closer to mystery; his spiritual sensitivity will bring greater harmony between his self-knowing and his knowledge of God; his spiritual knowledge will draw him into relationship with the gentle and humble heart of Jesus. When Jesus says, "learn from me; for I am gentle and humble in heart," he is inviting us into this relational way of coming to understanding.[4]

3. Matt 6:25–33.
4. Matt 11:29, *NRSV*.

TOWARDS ATTENTIVENESS: IMAGERY, METAPHOR AND STORY

The Bible, so rich in story, imagery, metaphor, poetry, prophecy, song, and wisdom, has a wonderful capacity to stir our emotions, enliven our imaginations, and guide us into our interior landscape, transforming us from the inside-out. When Jesus saw that people were perplexed by his constant use of parables, he responded:

> The reason I speak to them in parables is that "seeing they do not perceive, and hearing they do not listen, nor do they understand." With them indeed is fulfilled the prophecy of Isaiah that says:
>
> "You will indeed listen, but never understand, and you will indeed look, but never perceive. For this people's heart has grown dull, and their ears are hard of hearing, and they have shut their eyes; so that they might not look with their eyes, and listen with their ears, and understand with their heart and turn— and I would heal them."
>
> But blessed are your eyes, for they see, and your ears, for they hear. Truly I tell you, many prophets and righteous people longed to see what you see, but did not see it, and to hear what you hear, but did not hear it. [5]

5. Matt 13:13–16, *NRSV*.

To receive wisdom far greater than Solomon's,[6] a rich way of life beyond our imagining,[7] and a calling to eternal glory found in Jesus,[8] who is the very image and likeness of God brought close to us,[9] we need our eyes, ears, and hearts to be open to a realm that is beyond our grasp. Rather than confronting resistances in a direct manner, Jesus guides pilgrims towards revelation by illuminating their emotional world, along with their believing imagination,[10] through imagery, metaphor, song, and story.

GUIDING PILGRIMS TO DISCOVER THEIR OWN PARABLES AND METAPHORS

The challenge for companions is to guide pilgrims to attend to their experiences by way of their hearts, since the attributes of the mind will not enable them to venture very far. We may think we do a lot for pilgrims when we give their troubles a classification or a name, but we become like the disciples arguing between two opposing pathologies about why a man had been born blind. Jesus breaks through their rudimentary diagnosis when he says, "He was born blind so that God's works might be revealed in him."[11]

---

6. Matt 12:42.

7. Eph 1:18.

8. 1 Pet 5:10.

9. 2 Cor 4:4.

10. Eugene Peterson, in speaking about the importance of Biblical story in our faith formation, suggests these help to train "our believing imagination to think *narratively*, immersing the praying imagination in *earthiness*." Peterson, *Leap Over a Wall*, 2.

11. John 9:3, *NRSV.*

Likewise, if we open space for pilgrims to enter their interior landscapes, they can discover their own parables and discern God's work—the movement of grace—in their own lives. To go deeper will require us to accompany pilgrims through their fear and darkness, but "the God who said, 'Let light shine out of darkness,' [shines] in our hearts to give the light of the knowledge of the glory of God in the face of Jesus Christ."[12]

COMPANIONING MANDY: A TREE'S ROOTS

One pilgrim, whom I will call Mandy, spoke of how she loved the metaphor of trees used in scripture and was drawn to seeing herself as a tree planted by streams of water, yielding fruit in season,[13] and being like a tree replanted in Eden's garden, putting deep roots down near the river. These scriptures so encouraged her faith that she did not need to fear the demanding times of life and that she could still be fruitful, even in times of personal dryness and drought.[14] She visualized this tree in a garden, being watered from a spring that would never run dry.[15]

Mandy's tree reflected back to her what was going on "beneath the ground," as she would say, "in that deep root system that continues to grow even in the cold of winter." Her "inner roots needed to connect with that eternal spring," which had become, "the very source of nourishment," "the very source of life." Her tree responded differently to the

12. 2 Cor 4:6, *NRSV.*

13. Ps 1:3.

14. Jer 17:8, with the emphasis on Eden from *MSG.*

15. Is 58:11.

various seasons, as Mandy did to the different movements in her own life.

Mandy knew that not all of her roots found the life source, that some were drawing from brackish and bitter water. As she sat in prayer with her tree image, she began to notice that some roots she had thought to be strong and healthy had become stunted and entangled by the bitterness and resentment she had harbored and tried to conceal from herself. Crying, she pleaded to the source of life for forgiveness and asked God to prune these roots and unproductive branches. Mandy's attention was drawn back to Jesus' metaphor of the vine and the gardener as she felt the pain of his pruning.[16] "I did not realize how much life energy was being siphoned off by the roots of bitterness and resentment. This energy is now able to surge through parts of my tree that can be so much more fruitful, both for me and for others."[17]

A HOUSE OF MANY ROOMS

While Mandy used the metaphor of a tree to symbolize her own being, others may use the symbol of a house. The emergence of a house or dwelling place in our dream life or waking reflections can echo back the metaphorical structure of our inner landscape, often holding out invitations for our growth, wholeness, and for more abundant life. Etty Hillesum, a remarkable young Jewish woman, wrote an exquisite and deeply moving description using the metaphor of a house in her diary from the foreboding Westerbork

16. John 15:1–17.
17. John 15:5.

concentration camp, just prior to being transported to the gas chambers of Auschwitz:[18]

> And I thank you for the great gift of being able to read people. Sometimes they seem to me like houses with open doors. I walk in and roam through passages and rooms, and every house is furnished a little differently, and yet they are all of them the same, and every one must be turned into a dwelling dedicated to You, oh God. And I promise You, yes, I promise that I shall try to find a dwelling and a refuge for You in as many houses as possible. There are so many empty houses and I shall prepare them all for You.

The divisions and fragmentations of our interior world are often externally masked, with important parts of our self "walled-up" or partitioned-off. Jesus speaks of the difficulties of a house divided against its self,[19] but he himself presents in his own person a house of unity, with no split between the outside and inside, no inner rooms closed off, no defensive walls or keep-out signs. We may be inclined to shift our gaze away from Jesus' house, ashamed of the disarray within our own, yet he draws us to grow in unity by pointing to Mary of Bethany and inviting us to fill our house with the fragrance of the perfume she used to anoint his feet.[20] If our inner house is constricted, he might remind us that the place he prepares for us, his Father's house, has many rooms.[21]

18. Hillesum and Hoffman, *Etty Hillesum*, 205.
19. Matt 3:25; Luke 11:17.
20. John 12:3.
21. John 14:2.

Whatever is his response, it will be unique to the condition and need of our particular house, and he will ask us to be awake and attentive to the light he brings into our hallways, rooms, nooks, and crannies. He may suggest we find a trusted companion to explore with us, especially the inner rooms of trauma, overwhelming emotions, darkness, and fear, where Jesus is ever willing to manifest his presence.

COMPANIONING ALLAN: A HOUSE WITHOUT FOUNDATION

Allan dreamt of a multi-story house that did not have foundations or a ground floor, and he was startled by how accurately this dream reflected his rootlessness at that very period of his life. By being attentive to the content of this metaphor, Allan was drawn to put down more substantial roots and to take responsibility for areas of his life where he was over-dependent on others' support. As Allan prayerfully sat with this dream-parable, his eyes were opened to the ways he was projecting his unmet needs onto his parents. The metaphor of the house "woke" him up to the discontinuity between an inner and outer reality, and invited him to grow up, an insight that emerged from within, rather than from a surface-level conversation with someone else.

Prayer leads us towards intimacy with God's Spirit and expands our inner self-awareness. As we cry out to God with a poor and humble spirit,[22] grieving our losses, we encounter a Father who is all merciful, even with our shame.

---

22. Matt 5:3–5.

The parable of Allan's house emerged from the gentle inner stirring of God's Spirit, an unforced rhythm of grace.

By attending to this house metaphor, we can venture into inner hallways, unexplored internal rooms that might be dark and frightening, storage rooms or heavily barricaded cupboards in which we have hidden experiences of trauma, afflictive emotions, insecurities, or poor reflections of ourselves, in the hope that they would never again see the light of day. We may glimpse doorways inviting us into places of warmth and light, their thresholds blocked by innumerable obstacles that seem to prohibit our entry. We may even find signs of crumbling or deteriorating foundations.

COMPANIONING JULIA:
EXPLORING DARK PASSAGEWAYS

Julia did not come to companioning with the expressed intention of dealing with her inner division, but she was feeling very down, tearful, not sleeping well, and finding it increasingly difficult to stand up for herself when she needed to do so.

When I asked Julia what she needed to attend to, she said she did not know, but that "Only as I sit here, my tears are starting to flow." "Can you take a moment just to notice your tears as they begin to flow?" I asked, inviting her to look inwards, which is very different from asking if she knew where the tears were coming from. The tears, drawn from a little brook that bubbled close by Julia's inner dwelling, became the guide. She began to name and attend to some deeper feelings, subtle signposts along a pathway to the entry hall of her inner house. Tears, feelings, emotions, and body responses, when acknowledged and gently attended to, can guide us inward, towards the more spacious and integrated places of the heart. The companion does not need to say to Julia: "I wonder if there was a stage in your life that you need to explore to find out why you are feeling so down at the moment?" Being attentive to her tears opened Julia to honoring her story thread as it unwound before her. The metaphor of house was Julia's own discovery, and even though her dwelling appeared dark and foreboding, she resolved to explore further.

But on a number of occasions, she stumbled and drew back. My companioning response at one of these junctures was, "As you draw back from that passageway, what do you notice is happening for you?" "I'm feeling scared," she replied, "very scared." "Can you say more about "scared" as it begins to take hold of you?" "It's very dark, it's a black monster-like shape that is blocking the hallway, as though it doesn't want me to go any further." "Can you turn around and look straight at it?" I asked. "I think I can. Oh, the black shape has these big round reddish eyes that seem to be trying to threaten me or scare me more." "Can you eye-ball those eyes?" "Yes, I can," responded Julia. "What do you notice happens as you do that?" I enquired. "The eyes and the shape begin to shrink. In fact it has become very small and has just moved back to let me pass." Julia continued her exploration of the passageway. Together, we had just worked our way around resistance!

Unfamiliar inner rooms may contain trauma and wounding, and it takes great courage to visit them, as the darker hallways are guarded by sentries of fear, placed there by an overly self-protective ego that works hard to keep us well away from pain or the undesirable and compromising parts of our self. Julia needed courage to explore these inner places and to be attentive to what was emerging in front of her. Eventually, she was led to a back room in which the adolescent part of her had been barricaded.

Julia spoke negatively about the adolescent period of her life, when she had been a feisty, rebellious young person, always in trouble. Her active imagination joined with her recollection, feelings, and emotions to offer her an encounter with this young person. Her adult self sought to barricade and isolate her adolescent self within one of its more secure rooms, even wishing her dead. Right in the midst of this volatile confrontation, the spacious and forgiving love of Jesus extended the boundaries of Julia's heart, freeing her to release this imprisoned part of herself and to welcome this fugitive home. It was heart-rending to witness this movement and to realize how Julia had become far too passive and compliant as an adult, and needed the adolescent's energy to move towards wholeness. At the point of her greatest disunity, Jesus lifted the veil on the glory of his own unity, inviting Julia into inner transformation and freedom.

The reflective team that witnessed this companioning encounter found resonance within Julia's inner parable, which was her very own. One team member had instinctively taken off his shoes, realizing on later reflection that the threshold to Julia's inner dwelling had become holy ground.

DIFFERENT METAPHORS

In each of these stories we can see how differing metaphors and images are important for different pilgrims. The guide then stays with the metaphor that the pilgrim uses, as they seek to find room and a safe space in which they can name their fears and find the welcoming and healing presence of Jesus, who says "Fear not, for I am your light and your salvation."

7

Transforming Wounds into Windows

Burn that is for my healing!
Wound of delight past feeling!
Ah, gentle hand whose touch is a caress,
foretaste of heaven conveying
and every debt repaying:
killing, you give me life for death's distress.[1]

A STRETCHING HEART

SANDRA STARK, a companion, desired to reflect the love of Jesus to others by being "active in love," willing to set aside whatever she was doing to open a welcoming and safe space. With such a trustworthy and compassionate heart, Sandra was often in great demand by troubled pilgrims. Her co-workers were inspired by her capacity to nourish people's troubled hearts and blessed by the warmth of her generous and loving heart.

Though Sandra loved to serve her Lord and sought to imitate the stance and spirit that she witnessed in his

1. John of the Cross, *The Living Flame of Love, 2nd stanza*. Translated by Flower, *Centred on Love*, 22.

gospel encounters with people, over time her heart became stretched. Dark circles ringed her eyes, and she started putting on a lot of weight, almost as if she needed to store up love for others in her own body. Her attendance at home group, community prayer, and worship became irregular. When close friends asked about her relationship with the Lord, she confessed that she was spending less time in prayer and the Word, but was finding God in other people. Then she began to experience conflict with someone she had long supported and started to close herself off, as if she could give no more. Constantly anxious, irritable, and increasingly depressed, Sandra found sleep difficult and felt bitterly unappreciated for all the work she had done for others. Keeping her friends at arm's length, she felt angry and distant from God.

Though inspired by Jesus' love for others, with a desire to imitate him and join in his restorative mission, Sandra's wish to be "active in love" gradually eclipsed her commitment to be prayerfully reflective and intentional in her work. This shift can easily creep up on all who offer deeply of themselves in the service of others.

Like the Chinese character for the word crisis, which contains both "danger" and "opportunity," the companioning stance can be influenced by danger or opportunity, or it can creatively engage both until the real movement for healing and growth occurs. To hold such tensions requires the relational character of spaciousness coupled with a sacrificial relational dynamic. To creatively hold the "danger" in a life-giving way means that the reality of wounding, pain or suffering is not superficially diminished, but is walked through, even amidst counter-movements and points of resistance caused by fear, loss, grief, guilt, and shame.

FACING OUR POVERTY OF SPIRIT:
BURN THAT IS FOR MY HEALING![2]

In her dark hole, Sandra came face-to-face with her own inner emptiness and began to experience excruciating aloneness, grief, and disconcerting anger. When she finally allowed another discerning companion, Amy Appleton, to journey with her into this dark place, Amy encouraged Sandra to be attentive to her grief.

As Sandra began to speak about her anger and grief, Amy listened intently. After Sandra paused, she said, "Sandra, I wonder if you might go back to when you spoke of how your anger was beginning to bubble through. What was it like for you when you noticed it 'bubble through?'" This question enabled Sandra to become an active observer of her inner experience. Rather than feeling worried and preoccupied, Sandra moved toward the more spacious place of her heart, where she could witness her anger and, later, her deep sorrow. This was a long and painful journey, with Amy walking in solidarity alongside Sandra, even a little behind, but never in front.

ENCOUNTERING JESUS WHOSE TOUCH
IS A CARESS

In the midst of Sandra's encounter with grief, she had a fleeting glimpse of the presence of Jesus, and Amy asked, "Sandra, what did you notice happening to you as you caught that glimpse of Jesus?"

2. Matt 5:3–4

Sandra replied, "That he is with me right in the very midst of what is happening to me." Amy encouraged her to be attentive to this experience of Jesus' presence by keeping the grief-filled eyes of her mind and heart fixed on him.

Though initially hidden from Sandra, grace was working around the foundations of the protective walls she had built at various stages of her life to hide away unacceptable parts of herself and to protect herself from the accumulated pain of her past. Grace was loosening the grip of some of her compulsions and infusing her with the courage to face the source of her wounding and pain.

Amy's stance was gentle and relaxed as she stepped into the unknown, following the story thread as it emerged, encouraging Sandra to be attentive and reflecting back snippets of what she had said. Rather than offering analysis of what was emerging for Sandra, Amy placed absolute trust in the invisible hand of grace as it guided Sandra's story to the surface of her conscious awareness, untangling the threads one by one.

Though deeply touched by the grief and pain that pushed upward into Sandra's conscious awareness, and often feeling the heat of her own tears pressing against the back of her eyes, Amy remained calm and restful, knowing that this relational space needed to be kept safe and free of fear. She gave almost her whole attention to Sandra's words, gestures, emotions, and emerging revelations and insights, while at the same time heeding how her inner resonance was cueing into the submerged flows beneath Sandra's story. By attending to the subtle movements of grace, Amy became aware that they had crossed an important inner threshold and were edging towards a painful precipice.

In a tear-filled moment, within the safe and restful space that Amy had opened for her, Sandra saw a very young child. Active imagination and recollection had joined Sandra's feelings and spiritual sensitivities, inviting Sandra to re-experience a difficult and traumatic time in her childhood. Intuition and discernment joined with the adult part of Sandra to assist her in witnessing and making meaning of past events.

Out of the shadows came a little girl completely over-whelmed with the responsibility of caring for younger siblings and a very sick mother. Eventually, when all the work was done, the exhausted little girl retired to her bed to sob herself to sleep. Under her pillow was a fantasy story about the adventures of a happy, carefree little girl, which she would read on the occasions when she had a little more energy before sleeping. After a period of observing the child and sobbing along with her, the adult Sandra looked up at Amy and asked, "How could they even ask that of her? Who was caring for little Sandra?"

As a discerning companion, Amy noticed that Sandra had almost become the little child again and gently reflected back the question, "Who could care for little Sandra?"

"Not her mother; she was too sick," replied Sandra. "Not her father, because though he was a kind man, he had been very busy and preoccupied at the time." Then Sandra whispered, "Perhaps only God."

"Could you invite God to care for little Sandra?" asked Amy.

"Yes," answered Sandra in a voice that could barely be heard.

"What do you notice God is doing?" inquired Amy.

"It is Jesus," said Sandra, "and the little girl does not seem all that pleased to see him."

"She is not pleased to see him. Is there something that she might need to say to Jesus?"

"Little Sandra needs to ask him where he was when she was having to care for all those people," said Sandra.

"Could she do that?"

"Yes! She does." After a few moments Sandra began to speak again: "Jesus has knelt down and is telling the little girl that he was there for her and always has been. The little girl has climbed onto his lap and is resting her tired head on his chest. I think she has gone to sleep."

"Now that the child is settled, what would the adult Sandra like to ask of Jesus?" Amy inquired.

"I am asking Jesus what I need to do to rekindle the love for other people that I seem to have lost."

"What do you notice about his reply?" asked Amy.

"It is very strange," said Sandra. "He seems to be saying, just put all your energy into loving me. Do you think that is strange? He doesn't seem to be saying any more." Amy does not reply, but notices warmth and joy welling up inside.

WALKING ON HOLY GROUND: FORETASTE OF HEAVEN CONVEYING

As a companion, Amy encouraged Sandra to be with the experience of rest that came from her encounter with Jesus and the little child. When she sensed that this time was drawing to a close, she asked Sandra whether she would like to inwardly acknowledge the little child and Jesus.

A period of silence followed, during which both Sandra and Amy knew they had moved onto holy ground. Without hurrying Sandra, Amy asked if Jesus had prompted her towards a particular scripture. A beautiful smile lit up Sandra's face as she said, "'You shall love the Lord your God with all your heart, with all your soul, with all your mind, and with all your strength.... You shall love your neighbor as yourself.'[3] Now I get it. I have been trying to do the second without the first—all in my own strength, just like that little girl."

Relying on her own resources had become an ingrained resolve that Sandra had clung to for years, along with her conflicting ways of finding love. In letting go, this part of Sandra died.

In the safety of this companioning relationship, the wounding that Sandra had long ago hidden away had been exquisitely guided upwards by an unseen hand to the surface of her conscious awareness, where it was lovingly held by a trusted companion so that it could be explored and re-experienced. Amy was able to do this because her own wounds had been held in this way by Jesus, who in turn invited her to participate in his life and mission of restoration for a broken and suffering humanity. By companioning Sandra in this cruciform way of Jesus, Amy was able to hold the tension between the suffering, pain, and death that Sandra was experiencing, and the hope that a "resurrection," an opportunity for new and greater life, would follow.

Through Christ's sacrificial offering of himself and his journey through death and resurrection, Sandra's wound became a window through which she could become an

3. Luke 10:27.

active participant in the life of God, a living spring over-flowing with the love, grace, compassion, and heart of Jesus. Her wounding, which Christ transformed into sensitivity, knowing, and inner freedom, could now be offered to others, particularly those on the edges of her community whom she had never before dreamed of reaching.

8

Bidding the Soul Welcome[1]

Love bade me welcome, yet my soul drew back[2]

THE SPACIOUS HEART

WE ARE all aware when a person is completely at ease with us and extends genuine hospitality, listens with keen empathy and interest, does not judge us, and affords us real regard. When a person is being authentic to who they really are, they do not try to be someone they are not, nor intentionally hide behind false masks. We can also intuit when people have a good sense of humble self-awareness, for they do not have to be the centre of attention, nor act defensively in conversation, nor engage in blaming others, but are careful to focus on others, and intentionally open up space in conversations for those who are more reserved. Some people are more transparent than others, not because they wear their hearts on their sleeves, but in the way they reveal that what we see on the outside is congruent with

---

1. Adapted from the first line of George Herbert's poem, "Love bade me welcome." In Quiller-Couch. (ed.). *The Oxford Book*, No. 286.

2. "/ . . . Guilty of dust and sin." Ibid. Lines 1 & 2.

74

what is on the inside. We are drawn to such mature people and find them spacious, sensitive, and easy to trust.

QUICK-EY'D LOVE[3]

As we reflect on Amy Appleton's companioning in the previous chapter, we notice that rather than casting herself in the role of a detached expert, Amy integrated the relational capacities described above and offered her authentic, whole self in the service of Sandra. Carl Rogers describes such a process as "congruent" and suggests that, "The more the therapist is herself in the relationship, putting up no professional front or personal façade, the greater is the likelihood that the client will change and grow in a constructive manner."[4]

In the relationship between Amy and Sandra, Amy put her own concerns and needs aside to focus her attention on where Sandra was at that particular moment in time. This recalls the moment when the resurrected Jesus meets two downcast pilgrims on the road to Emmaus and asks, "What are you discussing with each other while you walk along?" One responds, "Are you the only stranger in Jerusalem who does not know the things that have taken place there in these days?" In spite of all that Jesus has just been through, he lays it aside in order to open unlimited space for them. In this incredible gesture of self-emptying, he only uses two words: "What things?"[5]

3. "But quick-ey'd Love, observing me grow slack / From my first entrance in," Ibid., Lines 3 & 4.

4. Rogers, *Carl Rogers*, 9.

5. Luke 24:17–19, *NRSV*.

In the beginning of our companioning work it can seem risky to bring our authentic, whole self into a relationship with a pilgrim, but this self-giving and other-receiving love mirrors the self-emptying of Jesus.[6] And as we saw with Amy, it opens a safe, restful, and calm space for the pilgrim to begin in a "dark hole" and from that place reveal the painful language, contradictory gestures, and wounded feelings that have been held tightly within.

Experience as a companion taught Amy that walking in true solidarity into places of pain and fear is personally destabilizing, so she does not claim to be whole and unified within herself, but humbly maintains that she is active in her own journey towards wholeness as she seeks to reflect and embody Jesus' authenticity, compassion, and sacrificial love, trusting that "He is in us as we are in him."[7] By embodying Jesus' wholeness, Amy was able to embrace Sandra's troubled and fragmented self, freeing Sandra to embark on her own journey of self-discovery as she explored the roots of her wounding. When Sandra reached her most painful threshold, Amy was fully present to accompany her through the door in truth with the forgiving, healing, and transforming love of the Trinity.[8] In spite of Sandra's fear and pain, Amy did not lose her moorings, but remained calm and centered so that Sandra could safely journey into the dark and fearful experiences hidden away in the deepest recesses of her person. In this way, Amy was willing to become poor so that Sandra might become rich and enter

6. Phil 2.

7. van Kaam and Muto, *Dynamics*, 42–43.

8. Eph 4:25.

God's glory.[9] When Jesus became manifest in the midst of this encounter, his presence blended seamlessly with Amy's, for she had embodied his invitation to: "Come to me, all you that are weary and are carrying heavy burdens . . ."[10]

LOVE'S SWEET QUESTIONING[11]

Rather than adopting an expert stance by offering sugges- tions, advice, analysis, or problem-solving, Amy joins with Sandra in a spirit of humility, encouraging Sandra to be at- tentive to what is emerging in front of her. She places trust in the life-giving power of a human relationship that reflects and embodies the wholeness of Jesus to evoke greater life from within the pilgrim.

Though Sandra was at the centre of Amy's focus throughout the encounter, there was an experience of mu- tuality in the communion that flowed between them, for Amy opened herself to the gift that Sandra would bring to her. The journey of pain, death, and resurrection resonated within Amy because, like Sandra, Amy had been deeply wounded and was still in need of ongoing healing and trans- formation. All companions are wounded healers in need of healing and transformation. As Amy later attended to the resonance she felt with Sandra in her own private place of prayer and reflection, she invited Jesus into the midst of it and emerged with a new experience of inner freedom. At the centre of the relational character and dynamic of com-

9. 2 Cor 8:9.

10. Matt 11:28, *NRSV*.

11. "Drew nearer to me, sweetly questioning / If I lack'd anything." Herbert in Quiller-Couch. Op cit., Lines 5 & 6.

panioning, there is a gift relationship, for just as Amy was a gift to Sandra, Sandra was also a gift to Amy, but Amy had to be open to receive the gift that Sandra had to offer her.

If we move our focus from Amy to Sandra, we remember that Sandra was also a companion who desired to be active in love in the way of Jesus. Yet at this point in her life and work, she had fallen into a "dark hole."

Stepping back a little from this encounter to look over Sandra's life, we discern that this episode is a vital part of her ongoing formation as a companion in the way of Jesus. It is clear from her earlier involvement in reaching out to others that she really desired to be formed in Jesus' way of love—his way of fully and sacrificially offering the whole of herself in the service of others. This gift, which emerged, in part, from her early experience of caring for her mother and her siblings, is also a place of significant wounding. Though Sandra has a great capacity for caring, there is a shadow side to her caring, which is brought into light as Sandra re-enters the place of wounding and pain.

Too early in life, Sandra was called upon to care for her mother and her siblings, making her rely upon her own resources. Through this early wounding she became convinced that she could only receive love and attention from her parents if she cared well for her siblings, and so she resolved to do so, whatever it cost. She projected this understanding of love onto her Heavenly Father, predicating her service and expressions of love for others on the belief that in order to receive love, she must first love others well.

Though hidden from view, these mixed motives worked their way into her companioning, creating a fracture within her that drew her back into the shadow or unacknowledged part of her inner life. She indicated later that, "it was like falling into a dark hole that seemed to have no way out."

LOVE'S WORTHY GUEST[12]

In a society that is concerned with expertise, status, technique, and achieving outcomes, it can be difficult to discern when this subtle slip into darkness begins. The diminishment of relational space between pilgrim and companion is one indication. When in solidarity and communion, the companion is open to receive the relational gift of the pilgrim for her own growth. However, when the companion is unable to recognize or receive this gift, the companion may have slipped into a stance of expertise, power, and status.

As humility, solidarity, and communion diminish, so does the companion's capacity to hold the pilgrim's wounding, pain, overwhelming emotions, and contradictions. Less capable of allowing space for self-exploration, inner healing, and growth, the companion may blame pilgrims for their predicaments and highlight their unresponsiveness and resistance when progress is slow. When companions cease to do their own reflective work and lose sight of their own counter-movements and points of inner resistance, pilgrims often encounter this unacknowledged resistance, slowing their progress.

The growing discontinuity between the change one is seeking in others and what is happening in oneself erodes personal authenticity, and the companion loses connections with her own inner moorings and slips into the shadow side

12. "'A guest,' I answer'd, 'worthy to be here'; / Love said, 'You shall be he.'" Ibid., Lines 7 & 8.

of her life. Having forfeited the life-giving and transforming power of love, fatigue will become more of a daily issue, often accompanied by an experience of being emotionally overwhelmed. The term "burn-out" has been aptly coined for trends when companions "burn up" parts of their self, including their capacity to love.

LOVE'S SMILING REPLY[13]

When we meet such cries for help and support with the response that it is an opportunity for capacity-building in personal ministry, this is gross negligence. Any response that denies access to the relational space in which real sharing, support, healing, and growth can occur is not reflective of the way of Jesus. Faith-committed companions are not exempt from these shifts into their shadow side, for inner fragmentation is often thinly papered-over by the rhetoric of "triumphant living" or "being in the light." In such cases, the action side of ministry in the name of Jesus is over-emphasized at the expense of the core relational dynamic of getting to know "the name" personally and intimately.

In solitude, quiet, and stillness, in obedient and attentive listening, in openness to the movement of the Spirit, we encounter the flow between our own person, the person of Jesus, and the community of the Trinity. Through intimacy with the Father and the Son, we become intimate with the person of our self, so that we can grow in authenticity, wholeness, and steadfastness. Within this loving and intimate encounter, we begin to understand a little of the

13. "Love took my hand and smiling did reply, / 'Who made the eyes but I?'" Ibid., Lines 11 & 12.

mystery of the Son, who never acted independently of the Father[14] and who could claim unequivocally that he and the Father were indeed of one heart and one mind.[15]

The quintessential challenge of engaging in the way of Jesus is the invitation to be formed by this same love and to participate actively in God. Our ongoing formation in companioning should be in complete harmony with our growth as followers of Jesus. Our active task is to deepen our experience of God by getting to know Jesus personally and intimately as the one who invites us into deeper relationship with, and active participation in, the life and love of God.[16]

The relational quality and dynamic of faith-committed companioning is found through our own participation with the relational essence and life-giving vibrancy of God, yet there is much to divert us. Love will bid us welcome as we enter seriously into our formation, but our soul might draw back.[17] This acknowledges that our desire to plunge into full participation in the way of Jesus will involve both forward movement and a resistant counter-movement, about which we will need to be prayerful, attentive, and reflective.

14. John 5:19.

15. John 10:30, *MSG*.

16. 2 Pet 1:3–4.

17. "Love bade me welcome, yet my soul drew back . . ." Herbert in Quiller-Couch. Op cit., Line 1.

9

Seeing into the Life of Things[1]

. . . and for him to see me mended
I must see him torn.[2]

A SAFE AND SACRED SPACE

THOSE WHO are engaged in interpersonal ministry often become afraid and retreat into their expert professional status when faced with the overwhelming suffering and pain endured by many pilgrims. As discussed in Chapter One, Martha reveals this tendency to shift into a stance of power when she seeks to co-opt Jesus' power to influence her sister: "Lord, do you not care that my sister has left me to do all the work by myself? Tell her then to help me."[3] But as we have seen, rather than taking Mary's side or colluding with Martha against Mary, Jesus creates a safe and spa-

---

1. "While with an eye made quiet by the power / Of harmony, and the deep power of joy, / We see into the life of things," lines from the poem, 'On Revisiting the Banks of the Wye During a Tour, July 13, 1798,' William Wordsworth, *Poetical Works*, 163.

2. The last two lines from Luci Shaw's poem, "Mary's Song", in Shaw, *Widening Light*, 43.

3. Luke 10:40, *NRSV*.

cious place where he can hold Mary's contradictions with grace and mercy, while at the same time calling her towards deeper truth.

Yet the quest for truth can easily stretch away from grace and mercy, as we have seen with the religious lawyer[4] in Chapter Six, and as we will see again in this chapter, when we examine the religious leaders' treatment of the woman they claim to have caught in the act of adultery.

SPACE FOR THE DIVINE TO SQUEEZE THROUGH

As Jesus is sitting down teaching people in the temple, the religious leaders bring in a woman accused of adultery and make her stand in front of everyone. Wanting to test Jesus so they could trap him and bring a charge against him, the religious leaders approach Jesus and say, "Teacher, this woman was caught in the very act of committing adultery. Now in the law Moses commanded us to stone such women. Now what do you say?"[5] With their classic scapegoat (an adulterous woman) and their watertight version of Moses' law, these guardians of "safe" religion are seeking to establish power over and cast out this enemy, Jesus, because he is flaunting the rules. Previously, he told religious leaders, "... it is easier for heaven and earth to pass away, than for one stroke of a letter in the law to be dropped."[6] Would he now uphold this law, or not?

4. Luke 10:25–37.
5. John 8:3–6, *NRSV*.
6. Luke 16:17, *NRSV*.

The secret lives of these religious leaders contrast markedly with the public exposure of the adulterous woman who, possibly stripped of her outer garments, stands exposed, guilty, and ashamed, afraid for her life and anticipating an agonizing death by stoning. If her accusers are right, the law does not offer her any room for hope, nor does the prospect of testing the law with another member of the religious "in group."

The crowd gathered to hear Jesus teach turn suddenly toward the exposed woman. Ignoring the men's question, Jesus bends down and doodles on the ground with his finger.[7]

Both the crowd and the hyped-up temple heavy weights wrest their titillated eyes away from the woman and lean forward, intrigued by what he is writing. Is it his verdict? the woman's death warrant? With Jesus' figure now the centre of attention, a small inner space opens up within the crowd. Humble and non-confrontational, Jesus' stance is below the men, perhaps on level with the woman, who might have collapsed or been thrown to the ground by her accusers.

Sensing that she is no longer the focus of attention, the woman glances at the stooped figure of Jesus writing with his finger in the dirt, her heart pounding as she wonders if he is writing her death warrant.

In the pause that Jesus creates by bringing the focus of attention onto himself, becoming the scapegoat, God's Spirit invites these temple men to attend to their deep inner longing for intimacy with the One who created them as well as the Law. With their focus on external religious practices,

7. John 8:6.

these men—who are teetering on the precipice of their own sexual addictions—have become blind to their own sinfulness, inner contradictions, and mixed motives. Their behavior is addictive in nature, because they have become overly attached to the structure and form of their particular religious practices, its certitudes, rules, and power to demand obedience.

Finally, Jesus straightens up and speaks: "Let anyone among you who is without sin be the first to throw a stone at her."[8]

Operating out of a forgiving and life-giving love, Jesus opens the space in which surrender is made possible by stooping down again and writing on the ground, giving the religious men the opportunity to change posture as they look at what he is writing. "Is he listing my sins?" they might be musing. In this tense moment, Jesus places his own body between danger and opportunity, life and death opening space for the Divine Presence to squeeze through.[9] He does not push aside, nor dismiss, nor underplay the woman's sinfulness, but takes the entire burden of it upon himself, into his own heart, his own body. As Jesus gives space for the truth of these men's inner contradictions to squeeze through their highly guarded and protective self-righteous filters, he transforms a death-making place into a life-giving space.

By inviting these men, who are used to exercising power over others, into this reflective place, Jesus tenderly

8. John 8:7, *NRSV*.

9. What the Australian poet Noel Davis describes as "a pause/ a gap in the human go/ where the Divine squeezes through," from the poem "A Pause." In Davis, *Fallow's Hundredfold*, 14.

draws them to the dangerous brink of the breach between forgiving love and law-imposing power, where there is no neutral ground. Trapped in the legalism of safe religion, these men will either react, by finding yet another scapegoat to distract themselves from their contradictions, addictions, and bondage to the law, drawing an even tighter boundary around themselves.[10] Or they will respond, surrendering to Christ's embodiment of forgiving love by moving towards relationships, love, grace, and mercy.

As the temple men turn inward and reckon with their "poverty of spirit"[11] before the One who holds truth, grace, and mercy in perfect unity, the older men begin to walk away first; then the younger ones finally get it and follow.

The woman, transformed from an object into an on-looker, feels her senses slowly come to life as she watches the men's feet shuffle away, stilling the ring of their accusations.

Standing up, Jesus invites the woman to look up from her position in the dirt and meet his gentle gaze. As the Master Companion, he is careful to focus her attention on what has unfolded before her: "Woman, where are they?"

To a woman who is, perhaps, trembling and confused, turned utterly inside-out, those words dispel her doubt that the men seeking her violent destruction have gone. Jesus then asks the woman to reflect further on their departure with the question: "Has no one condemned you?"

---

10. We will witness this approach later in the gospel, and it will eventually lead to Jesus' death.

11. Matt 5:3.

Desperate to be freed from the deathly trap in which she might yet be caught by this religious teacher, the woman replies, "No one, sir."

And from within the One who embodies God's forgiving and enduring love, the One who holds mercy, grace, and truth in perfect unity, comes the remarkable response, "Neither do I condemn you."[12]

This steadfast "I" previously said "no" to the temptation of exercising power over others with the words: "Away with you, Satan! for it is written, 'Worship the Lord your God, and serve only him.'"[13] Jesus' pardon completely eclipses the power and death of the ones seeking to harm the woman. Her petrified mind is "made quiet by the power / Of harmony, and the deep power of joy," as she rests within his presence.[14]

In the absence of condemnation, and in the flow of forgiving love with the One who has come not to abolish the law but to fulfill it,[15] Jesus moves beyond a pardon and embrace of the woman before him by inviting her to turn around, a metanoia that frees her to choose a way of deeper rest and more abundant life than she has ever known or imagined possible: Go your way, and from now on do not sin again.[16]

To be freed from her relationship addiction, she will need to move away from poor sexual attachments towards deeper intimacy with the One who created her. To cross the

12. John 8:10–11, *NRSV*.

13. Matt 4:10, *NRSV*.

14. Wordsworth, *Poetical Works*, 163.

15. Matt 5:17.

16. Matt 4:10, *NRSV*.

threshold of her narrow existence and see anew "into the life of things,"[17] she will need to enter into obedient, listening communion with the One who loves her.

Looking ahead, we can anticipate the high price that Jesus will pay for the relational space he opens to this woman in these volatile minutes—a space he also extends to those who were witnesses, including the religious leaders, perhaps a small handful of whom turned their hearts towards Christ's forgiving love when they said "no" to the temptation of exercising power over another.

WITH THE EYE OF THE HEART MADE QUIET

As we bring this story into the companioning room, we might reflect on how Jesus brings his invitation to "Come . . . all . . . and I will give you rest . . . for your souls" into the volatile and hostile encounter in the temple, extending it to the accused and oppressed as well as the accuser and oppressor. Into the dark, constrained place of the religious leaders' addictive, oppressive, contradictory religious and cultural practices, Jesus offers all whom he encounters a loving embrace and a restful space in the presence of his gentle and humble heart.

Many pilgrims bring accusations against people who have wronged them into the companioning room, but in this story, Jesus shows us how not to collude, one party against another, but to stand firmly in the pathway of peace, even as we listen to and hold the criticisms, blame, projections, entanglements, and inner contradictions of the pilgrim. To avoid becoming parental, distantly professional or

17. Wordsworth, *Poetical Works*, 163.

powerfully directive, we will need to embody the spacious and gracious capacity of Jesus as we accompany pilgrims inwards to engage the truth of their wounded pasts and self-protective resolves.

For as we can learn from our Lord in this tense narrative from the gospel of John, we, too, can create a non-judgmental space, where pilgrims can share their stories without reservation or fear of rejection or condemnation. As companions, we then hold these burdens, contradictions, and entanglements close to the gentle and humble heart of Jesus, where there is no shame or condemnation, but only life-giving and forgiving love—the same love that is embracing our own addictions, burdens, and entrapments. And as we share in the flow of this love, we journey alongside the pilgrim towards the figure of a stooped-down liberator writing on the ground, fearlessly proclaiming "the good news of the Kingdom of God."[18]

18. Luke 4:43, *NRSV*.

10

Light Shall Arise into the Darkness[1]

If I say, "Surely the darkness shall cover me,
and the light around me become night,"
even the darkness is not dark to you;
the night is as bright as the day,
for darkness is as light to you.[2]

THE HOSPITAL AS COMPANIONING ROOM

IN THIS chapter we are witnesses to the encounter between Stephen Smith, a hospital pastoral care worker (companion), and David Davison, a patient (pilgrim) recovering from a massive heart attack, who has been referred by the doctor for pastoral care.

The chart hooked over the hospital bed railing identified David as a fifty-year-old "minister of religion" who had been healthy before the heart attack. Though his vital signs were satisfactory after a successful by-pass surgery, the physiotherapist noted the slowness of David's rehabilitation, his lack of enthusiasm, and his disinterest in food. "Query

1. Ps 112:4.
2. Ps 139:11–12, *NRSV.*

depression," he had written in the file, but a formal referral to the consultant psychiatrist had not yet been made.

When Stephen Smith first encountered David, he gently introduced himself and explained his role as a pastoral care worker. Without showing his face, David mumbled into the bed sheets, "Thank you for coming, but I'm really not up to talking today."

"You are saying you are not up to talking today," Stephen replied. "I can drop-by tomorrow."

David had grown used to the bustle of staff, all of whom could be polite, but they often had to go on with their tasks even if you offered a small protest. He twisted his head around and brought his left eye above the arm that cradled his head so that he could catch a glimpse of this man standing next to his bed, as if waiting to be dismissed. "OK," David said, and took a second glance at Stephen before withdrawing his head back into its protective shell.

Stephen lingered a moment to rest his gaze on David's partially hidden body. The eye of Stephen's heart had been quick to discern the pain etched on David's fleeting face, and he prayed silently, "Come, Lord Jesus, come." His eyes fixed on the back of David's head, Stephen said, "Look forward to visiting with you tomorrow," and walked away.

After Stephen left, David felt bad that he had dismissed a fellow minister so rudely, but as his remorse faded, he realized that he had spoken the truth. He really wasn't up to talking. How could he possibly talk about the alarming flood of negative, destructive, nightmarish thoughts that had been recklessly racing through his mind—first under anesthetic, then in drug-induced delirium, now in nightmares and through the wakeful anxiety that plagued him all day long? The partially closed curtain around his bed and the sheets and blankets over his body did little to suppress the inner darkness that engulfed David, leaving him uncertain if there was anything to live for.

Though he had never cried before, tears suddenly seemed to flow up from a very dark, deep well within him. Though he had known of this dark place in the past, he had always kept moving, first putting all of his energy into the small business he had founded in a desperate attempt to receive approval from his demanding and perfectionist father. Then, after experiencing a remarkable conversion at the age of thirty-five and attending theological college, he became a highly committed, energetic pastor with a highly infectious passion for God and a love of doctrine. But the restfulness and steadfastness of Jesus kept eluding him as his compulsion and drive to keep running continued from one year to the next. Now, completely immobilized on a hospital bed with a failing heart, David found himself unable to work for people's approval, unable to strive to please God, and too tired to keep running away from his inner darkness and turmoil.

SURELY THE DARKNESS SHALL COVER ME

The next day, when Stephen arrived, David turned slightly toward him, exposing just a little of his tear-stained face, but as his eyes met Stephen's, he glanced away and said, "I'm not much good for company. I don't have anything to say."

After Stephen greeted David, he sat down in the chair beside the bed and reflected back what David had said: "You are saying that that you don't feel as though you are good company and that it is just like there is nothing left to say." David grunted his affirmation. After a pause, Stephen said: "Do you mind if I just sit here quietly for a few minutes. When it is like there is nothing left to say, there is no need to say anything."

David found this response strangely reassuring, so he replied, "Sure. That's okay, if you have time to stay for while." Stephen accepted this invitation.

Over the next ten minutes, nothing more was said, apart from Stephen's brief signal that he was leaving and that he would like to return the next day and sit some more. After Stephen left, David sighed and noticed that he felt a little bit more relaxed. While Stephen had been sitting next to him, the bombardment of thoughts had stilled a little, though now they were beginning to battle for his attention with the words he had spoken to Stephen, and which Stephen had brought back to him: "I don't have anything left to say."

As David repeated these words, "I don't have anything left to say," over and over, the flow of negative thoughts retreated to mere background noise. "I was a person who used to have a lot to say," mused David as he thought about his widespread reputation as a Bible teacher, Old Testament lecturer, "defender of the faith," and keen articulator of doctrine, "but now I don't have anything left to say."

Lying on his back, his hands supporting the back of his head, David stared at the ceiling, trying to remember his favorite lecture on the book of Leviticus, but the pages of his memory were as bare as the walls of his hospital ward. He pictured the bulging filing cabinets in his office, but when he imagined himself opening them, he saw that they were completely empty, as if everything that he had written over the years had evaporated from his memory. "I don't have anything left to say." With a groan, David rolled back into his pillow and wept bitter tears.

THE LIGHT AROUND ME BECOME NIGHT

The next morning, after a fitful sleep, David began to look forward to seeing Stephen again as he recalled the respite he had felt during and after Stephen's visit. But his anticipation was laced with dread that he would share with Stephen the words and images of death and destruction that had plagued him through the long, dark night.

When Stephen arrived, David greeted him and raised himself to a half-sitting position, hiding his clenched, trembling hands beneath the bedcovers, as if to still the unspeakable thoughts he had trapped inside. As Stephen sat down beside him, David talked about his heart attack and slow recovery, looking away from Stephen as he spoke and quickly brushing away the tears that slipped out of his eyes.

Though quiet, Stephen watched over David, seeking to be available to him rather than trying to analyze him. He resonated with the turmoil, pain, and grief he sensed within David, but did not ask probing questions or press him to speak.

With this sensitive, gentle man sitting beside him, David noticed that his hands were more relaxed, though he kept them hidden beneath the covers. He was relieved that Stephen seemed comfortable with his silence and tears, and he felt calm and restful in his presence.

In the peace that remained for the hour after Stephen left, David found that he could distance himself from his distressing inner thoughts to watch them, as if they were a slowly passing parade of voices calling for his demise. "We knew you would never amount to much, David," they taunted. "We knew you'd fail us. Look at you now with your broken heart. You'd be better off dead." Folding in on himself to escape from the clamoring voices, David heard the faint cry of a frantic child and felt completely abandoned and alone. Burying his face in his pillow, he groaned and wept violently until a sedative injection carried him, falling, over the edge of a deep, dark hole.

CONSUMED BY DARKNESS

The next day, sitting up in bed beside Stephen, David was startled to hear himself sharing this sensation with his companion. "You say that you remember having that injection and then it was like falling into a deep dark hole," Stephen said in his quiet voice, such a respite from the destructive thoughts that had ravaged David through each of his long nights in the hospital.

"Yes. That is what I remember," David said, looking into Stephen's gentle blue eyes, which welcomed him into the safe, restful, and non-judgmental presence of this companion.

"As the memory of that deep dark hole returns to you now, what do you notice about it?"

"It seems to be inviting me to enter and explore it," David said.

"What would it be like to enter and explore that hole?"

"It would be very scary," David said, hesitating. "I am not sure if I could do it."

"Scary," repeated Stephen. "Could you say more about 'scary?'"

David shuddered as though something powerful had grabbed and shaken him.

"What did you notice just happened to you?"

"My thoughts seemed to take over," David whispered, afraid to say more.

"As your thoughts try to take over, what is that like for you, when they want to take over?"

"My heart starts to pump faster, my chest tightens, and something seems to be stuck in my throat." David's hand moved up to hold his throat. "I am worried that I won't be able to breathe."

Stephen moved his hand over his own heart, his chest, and his throat. "Your heart pumps faster, your chest tightens, something seems to stick in your throat and you worry that you won't be able to breathe."

"I actually can still breathe. But this thing in my throat!" He held his throat. "I almost feel I'm going to vomit." His face contorted in distaste.

"What do you notice about the vomit?" Stephen asked calmly.

"I know I'm not going to vomit, but I can see what needs to come out—a black poison mass."

"Can you keep observing that black poison mass?"

"I could see it clearly, but my thoughts have distracted me." David clenched his trembling hands and thrust them under the covers.

"As those thoughts now come, David, what do you notice about them?"

David glanced at Stephen, then he stiffened and turned away. "I can't say what those thoughts are."

"Without saying what they are, can you slow them down and watch each one as it comes?"

David sighed in relief. "Yes. I can look at them one by one."

"As you do that, where is your attention being drawn?"

"There is a big dark shape that wants to control everyone else."

"As you look at that dark shape, what begins to happen for you?"

"I feel scared." David swallowed. "You know, Stephen, that black shape is my fear."

"Can you keep looking directly at fear?" Stephen's eyes, fixed upon David's, were strong and unwavering.

"Fear has stirred-up the others, and they're beginning to shout again." David closed his eyes and swallowed. "As I look at those big, red, bloodshot eyes, fear is shrinking—it's so small I could pick it up in my hand."

"What would it be like to do just that, David, to pick it up and ask it about its real concern?"

David's focus drew inwards. "Fear told me that he has been trying to protect me, but it's been hard to get my attention unless he's negative. He's convinced my old life-style will totally destroy me, which I can understand now. But why have my thoughts been so dark, negative, and destructive in the weeks since my heart attack?" David held his head in both hands, utterly exhausted. "I thought I needed to die," he sobbed.

"The place you have been in over these past weeks has been so totally dark that you thought that you needed to die," responded Stephen, feeling the hot sting of tears in his eyes as he held the overwhelming weight of David's sorrow in his own heart.

EVEN THE DARKNESS IS NOT DARK

In the sessions that followed, David and Stephen traveled together into the darkest places of David's deepest wounding. The cry of the lost child guided them to an inner cavern, where David came face to face with this little boy, who had grown up believing that he could only gain the love and approval of his parents through his hard work and achievements.

Clothed in the gentle, humble, restful, spacious heart of Jesus, Stephen did not offer words of counsel, verbal expressions of comfort, affirmation, or advice to David about his predicament and fears. Rather he encouraged David to be attentive to what was happening within him and opened a spacious place within which David could journey into the dark and painful realms of his inner landscape, where the Spirit of Jesus could meet him and minister to his many deep wounds.

As David remained attentive to what was visually emerging in front of him, a deeper truth became manifest in the presence of Jesus, who lovingly accepted and embraced the little boy for who he was. As this presence lingered, the adult David was given a glimpse into his own father's deeply wounded heart and became privy to what had led to the demands that his father had placed upon him. At that moment, David felt an inner shift, accompanied by an experience of grief for the little boy and his father, and a flow of love, compassion, and forgiveness towards his father.

THE NIGHT IS AS BRIGHT AS THE DAY

In spite of David's inner growth and newfound freedom, the deep grief remained about his lost ministry. Stephen encouraged him to stay with this lament. "What are you noticing, David, when you say the words: My whole ministry is over?"

Tears filled David's eyes. "There is nothing left for me to live for, nothing."

"Nothing left for you to live for." After a long silence, Stephen asked, "What are you noticing now, David?"

"I'm in a very dark place. There is no light. I'm completely alone. It is very cold. I just don't know what to do."

"You're in a dark place. There is no light. You are completely alone. It is cold. And you are saying you don't know what to do."

David felt strangely comforted in hearing his experience echoed back to him. As Stephen encouraged David to be attentive to the dark, cold place he was in, David began to notice a glow of light. As he moved to explore it, he told Stephen that this light contained some warmth.

"What is that warm light inviting you to, David?"

"To reach out," David replied.

"As you reach out, David, what do you notice?"

"I don't see anything different, but I hear the word, 'Come.'"

"You hear the invitation to come," said Stephen.

At the point when there was nothing left to live for, David heard this word of invitation, and in an instant, he felt a flow of warmth through his body as a breeze stirred the curtains and caressed his cheeks.

Stephen sat prayerfully at David's bedside, witnessing this outpouring of grace and rest by the Divine Companion.

FOR DARKNESS IS AS LIGHT

Until that day, David had only heard Jesus' invitation to "Come . . . and . . . rest"[3] as an invitation to others who were troubled, weary, and burdened, those who really needed the Lord's grace. Though he had worked hard to minister in the name of Jesus, he had never been truly intimate with the person of Christ. But with the failure of his physical heart and the collapse of the scaffolding that had propped up his identity, David's persona—the mask that his ego had crafted to make him care about his reputation as a successful minister and to seek praise from those around him—had been shattered. Later, David was able to reflect that his suffering had freed him to relinquish his crippling need for approval, not only from his family and the people around him in ministry, but also in the way he projected his father's exacting demands onto God.

3. Matt 11:28, *NRSV.*

When suffering rendered a fissure in David's drive and self-reliance, the Divine squeezed through the gap and light shone right into the darkness. Jesus beckoned to David, and David responded with the whole of his physically broken heart, troubled mind, tortured spirit, and weary soul, opening himself to receive the gifts of God. Implanted with a renewed sense of God's abiding presence, David could now grow up from the inside out in the knowledge and love of God and in Jesus' life and restorative mission in the world.[4] As David now companions other pilgrims along the way of Jesus, he journeys in tune with the unforced rhythms of God's grace.[5]

---

4. Col 1:10.
5. Matt 11:29, as expressed in *MSG*.

11

Like a Peasant Called Before a Great King

If I did not understand
the glory and sufferings of the human heart,
I would not speak before its holiness.
Like a peasant called before a great king,
when all of his court is assembled
that is how I stand before every woman and man.[1]

BEFORE THE GLORY AND SUFFERINGS
OF THE HUMAN HEART

WHEN MARJORIE Meyer, a serenely beautiful and dignified eighty-year-old, enters the companioning room, she always offers a word of encouragement and a genuine inquiry concerning my well-being. A woman of prayer and social action, Marjorie lives among people with great needs in a context of scarcity, stretched to a breaking point in her care for others. Yet there is no meagerness in Marjorie's soul, which is nourished daily as she sups the body and blood of her Lord and participates intimately in

---

1. From Catherine of Siena's poem, "A Peasant before a King." In Ladinsky, *Love Poems*, 207.

the community of the Trinity, whose love throbs through her spacious heart.

Once she is resting comfortably in the armchair opposite me, Marjorie speaks slowly and softly, drawing her words and images from a deep inner pool that she has been reflecting upon and praying over, inviting me to step with her into an excruciating moment of decision, where to choose one way will generate angst and certain criticism, but to choose the other is like an anguished death.

Reflecting each choice back to Marjorie, I extend my left hand as if to hold the first option and my right hand to hold the second, and feel a strong burning pain in the region of my heart.

Expressing gratitude for the advice she's received from friends and other advisors, Marjorie pauses and says, "But do they really know the depths and pain of a mother's heart?"

The burning sensation intensifies within me, and the open palms of my hands are drawn further apart.

"I usually have an idea of where God is inviting me, but this time He seems to be silent," Marjorie continues, unselfconsciously wiping the tears from her eyes with a handkerchief.

I breathe spaciousness into her receptive heart, trusting God to guide her along the pathway of peace. "What is it like to be in that place of decision and experience God's silence?"

Marjorie speaks of feeling as if she were being "torn" in two, and again I notice that I have stretched my hands even further apart. Pondering the next question for some time before speaking, I ask, "You said before that God seemed to be silent on the decision that is in front of you. I wonder if you would notice where Jesus might have experienced something of the "torn" that is now happening with you."

"He is on the cross," Marjorie says quietly, then emphatically, "Yes! He is on the cross."

My arms extend further to the sides, symbolizing the cross. "Yes! You are noticing he is on the cross."

As I fold my hands in my lap and rest, Marjorie says, "Thank you! I know exactly where I am now. Thank you very much for that." She smiles, gathers her things, rises to her feet, and kisses me farewell.

SILENT, BEFORE HOLINESS

After she leaves, I return to my companioning chair for a time of prayerful reflection, feeling stunned at the magnitude of our brief time together and how quickly the session finished once Marjorie's inner gaze returned to the memory of her crucified Lord. With the guidance of the Spirit, who came alongside to answer her heart-felt cry at feeling forsaken, Marjorie slipped past the protective sentries guarding her heart from the pain of God's seeming absence and was drawn by the Paraclete to the foot of the cross, the listening post for all stories of human brokenness and suffering, where love, pain, joy, and sorrow can mingle and be held as one. And where, regardless of how she chose to resolve her dilemma, her exile ended.

For as she connected the reality of her overwhelming experience of being "torn" with the torn body of her Lord, she knew she was drinking from her Lord's cup, just as she had earlier that morning at her local church. And in the security and restfulness of her crucified Lord's presence, she knew she was held by Emmanuel, God with her, in whom all manner of things would be well, and the light of Christ, the resurrected One, burned brightly within her once again, illuminating the inner knowing of her soul.[2]

Marjorie was certainly not seeking advice, nor was she looking for my assistance in problem-solving, for I was not even privy to the resolution that unfolded before her as the Spirit re-oriented her compass toward Christ, her rock. Instead, she was seeking a relational presence reflective of the welcome, humility, and gentleness of Jesus. As her gaze rested upon him, I had to move out of the way, that she might find the ultimate truth: that Christ was life for her and would, through his easy yoke and light burden, guide her soul to rest.[3]

Walking alongside such a holy pilgrim draws me again towards the priestly and sacramental heart of companioning: to cooperate humbly with the stirrings of grace as the truth-seeking Spirit guides both pilgrim and companion into a sacred and restful sanctuary, where the pilgrim might be attentive to their deeper story, and the companion stands silent, humbled by the glory, sufferings, and holiness of the human heart.

2. Echoing Julian of Norwich. In Manton, *The Gift of Julian of Norwich*, 4.

3. Matt 11:28–30.

12

Proclaiming the Year of the Lord

Six days before Passover, Jesus entered Bethany where Lazarus, so recently raised from the dead, was living. Lazarus and his sisters invited Jesus to dinner at their home. Martha served. Lazarus was one of those sitting at the table with them. Mary came in with a jar of very expensive aromatic oils, anointed and massaged Jesus' feet, and then wiped them with her hair. The fragrance of the oils filled the house.

Judas Iscariot, one of his disciples, even then getting ready to betray him, said, "Why wasn't this oil sold and the money given to the poor? It would have easily brought three hundred silver pieces." He said this not because he cared two cents about the poor but because he was a thief. He was in charge of their common funds, but also embezzled them. Jesus said, "Let her alone. She's anticipating and honoring the day of my burial. You always have the poor with you. You don't always have me."[1]

---

1. John 12:1–8, *MSG*.

THE KINGDOM OF GOD HAS COME NEAR[2]

IN THIS penultimate chapter, we return our attention to the household of Mary, Martha, and Lazarus for a dinner party given in Jesus' honor. This gospel story is filled with the presence, glory, and fragrance of the coming kingdom, but also with counter-movements to the kingdom way.

On the occasion of Jesus' first visit as an honored guest in this household (Chapter One: Passing under the low lintel),[3] we remember Mary's receptivity in contrast to Martha's reactive posture. At this second dinner gathering, we now see Mary's receptivity in Martha. Though little is said other than, she "served," this is in marked contrast to her actions and attitudes on the earlier occasion. Her service here is an expression of transformed personhood, for she now serves as an honoring of her Lord, "the Messiah, the Son of God, the one coming into the world."[4] Having witnessed her beloved brother move from life to death and then from death to life, Martha knows Jesus intuitively and experientially as "the resurrection and the life."[5]

Using this gospel story to illuminate the companioning encounters in the previous chapters, we see how the guide-companions have participated in the restorative work of Jesus, proclaiming the year of the Lord[6] and his coming kingdom within each of the pilgrim's particular worlds.

2. Mark 1:15, *NRSV.*
3. Luke 10:40.
4. John 11:27, *NRSV.*
5. John 11:25, *NRSV.*
6. Luke 4:19.

CASTING SHADOWS UPON HOLY GROUND

The reactive resistance we saw previously in Martha's "shadow side" is located in this gospel account within the attitudes and actions of Judas, who is also a guest at this banquet table. His discordant and challenging questions, noted parenthetically in this gospel narrative, reveal a constrained and conflicted heart that is becoming prone to accusations, deceit, and treachery.[7]

As Mary worshipfully anoints Jesus, pouring expensive perfume on his feet and wiping them with her hair, making the very ground upon which they recline holy, Judas declares, "'Why was this perfume not sold for three hundred denarii and the money given to the poor?' (He said this not because he cared about the poor, but because he was a thief; he kept the common purse and used to steal what was put into it.)"[8]

But as witnesses to Judas's protest, we might acknowledge that we, too, often utter such disclaimers in the face of "life," making distinctions about what is reasonable and prudent, tolerable, and just, or arguing about scarcity. After all, we have to look after our own! God helps those who help themselves! We may even wax eloquent about a needy group of people, as Judas does here with the poor. Even love can be considered a scarce commodity, for most of our deeper wounding has to do with our relationships. Judas' position in this story not only conveys our subtle resistance, but also exposes our underlying motives.

7. John 12:6.
8. John 12:5–6, *NRSV.*

Like the lawyer who comes to test Jesus, we may become lopsided as our religious legalism drifts away from grace and mercy. Or, like the accusers of the adulterous woman, we may fall into self-righteousness and neglect the contradictions that simmer just below the surface. Or like Jesus' own disciples when they come to the well and see Jesus talking with "that kind of woman," we may react out of judgment and fear rather than mercy and love.[9]

A shadow-side was also woven into the fabric of the companioning stories we witnessed between Andrea and Carol (in chapter three), Amy and Sandra (in chapters seven and eight), and Stephen and David (in chapter ten). In fact, such deep companioning is sometimes referred to as "shadow work." There is even a flicker of shadow in Marjorie's story (chapter eleven), which momentarily draws her gaze away from Christ, her crucified and resurrected Lord.

As Jesus makes clear, our newfound freedoms as we move towards deeper and more abundant life will not be applauded by all.[10] In fact, for many who witnessed Lazarus' resurrection prior to this banquet, the flow of life within Jesus was far too threatening, particularly among the religious leaders who were seeking his demise.[11] As we see with Judas, the thread drawing him to react and work against the grace of Christ is a tangled mass of accusations, lies, and fears, leading him towards despair and death.

9. John 4:27, *MSG*.
10. Matt 5:10–12.
11. John 12:9–11.

COME TO ME:
WALKING THE WAY OF THE CROSS

When Mary anoints Jesus' feet with perfume, Jesus praises her act of love and gratitude for anticipating and honoring the day of his burial: "Leave her alone. She bought it so that she might keep it for the day of my burial. You always have the poor with you, but you do not always have me."[12]

Because of Lazarus' previous death and resurrection, this household is already painfully aware of the cruciform passage, through death and burial, to Jesus' invitation to greater and more abundant life. In his reconciling presence at the banquet table, their hearts most likely hold both gratitude and sorrow, joy and pain as they anticipate the reality of his coming absence, to which he gently points them. And yet they also know, intuitively and experientially, that his burial and death will somehow open the fuller and more abundant life of his kingdom rest to them.[13]

As we have seen in the stories of Carol, Sandra, David, and Marjorie, as well as the woman accused of adultery, her accusers, and the Samaritan woman, Jesus extends his wide, "Come to me," embrace to all of humanity, both the wounded and the transformed, the torn and the mended, those living as shadows and those walking in the light. Within the spaciousness of the pierced heart of Jesus—his self-giving, and other-receiving love—there is room for Judas and Mary alike to find shelter and be reconciled. By taking upon himself both the enmity of Judas and the adoration of

---

12. John 12:7–8, *NRSV*. See also, John 12:7, *MSG*.
13. Matt 11:29, *NRSV*.

Mary, Jesus anticipates the way of the cross set before him, in order "that they may all be one."[14]

To be "in Christ" is to be embraced and enfolded in this sacrificial, self-giving and other-receiving love. As guides and companions of his way, we are to be agents of this grace to other pilgrims. The companions we met in the previous chapters extend this relational space to the pilgrims who come to them for guidance. We will briefly review how Andrea, Amy, and Stephen reflect this Trinitarian interflow of love to Carol, Sandra, and David.

ANDREA: GENTLE AND HUMBLE IN HEART

Had Andrea been reclining at the banquet with Jesus, she would have been profoundly moved by Mary's actions, which would have kindled within her a desire to pour out herself in the honor and service of her Lord. Her humility may have hidden how her response to Carol was just as fragrant an offering of kingdom life and love as Mary's.

Rather than defending herself from Carol's pain, distress, contradictions, and resistance, Andrea embraced Carol with the spacious heart of Christ, extending Jesus' invitation to "Come . . . and find rest," to her. By inwardly resonating with Carol's tumult and pain, Andrea embraced Carol with the "roominess" of the Triune Heart, mirroring back the inner resourcefulness, beauty, and image of God at Carol's deepest core.

As an agent of grace, Andrea trusted Christ to draw her into the heart of the Triune God each day as she lov-

14. John 17:31, *NRSV.*

ingly tended her relationship with him.[15] Had she been at
the banquet table with Mary and Martha, she would have
noticed and affirmed their intimacy with Jesus, as she often
encouraged other guides and companions to give this relational intimacy priority over the strategies of psychology
and the other social and behavioral sciences, essential as
these are.

AMY: LEARNING THE UNFORCED
RHYTHMS OF GRACE

Had Amy been at the banquet table, she would have been
quick to discern the golden thread of grace that wove its
way through Mary's fragrant offering, anticipating the
connection to Jesus' burial day. If we look closely at Amy's
companioning work, we notice that she faithfully tended
Sandra's emerging story thread. Rather than offering "outside" observations or analysis about what might be happening for Sandra, Amy encouraged Sandra to be attentive to
what was emerging directly in front of her, moment-by-
moment, trusting the pilgrim to know her own story best.
She also trusted that the presence of Jesus and the life of the
kingdom was close at hand,[16] and so encouraged Sandra to
be awake and attentive to this kingdom presence within her,
right in the midst of her suffering and pain.[17]

15. 2 Pet 1:3, *MSG*.
16. Matt 3:2.
17. Luke 17:21, Matt 25:13.

STEPHEN: FINDING HOPE
IN THE FACE OF DARKNESS

If Stephen were at this banquet table, I would not be surprised if he pondered the context of the gathering, six days before the Passover, reminding him that Easter was only so many days away as he ventured with David, who had nothing to live for and nothing more to say, into the darkest depths of his story. To be a companion in the way of Jesus, Stephen knew he had to locate David's story in the story of Jesus' suffering, death, burial, and resurrection.

Stephen would also have been aware of the fact that during this dinner party, the religious authorities were plotting against Jesus, whose teaching and kingdom living was drawing followers towards greater and more abundant life, threatening the powers of accusation, destruction, and death.

Along with Amy, Stephen discerned and cooperated with the golden threads of grace amidst David's wounding, trusting the manifest presence of Jesus and his restored kingdom life to break into his darkness and despair.

MARJORIE: FINDING REST FOR HER SOUL

Just as Mary of Bethany draws our focus to the feet of Jesus as she anoints them and wipes them with her hair, so Marjorie returns us to the feet of Jesus as he hangs on the cross. In the presence of this older pilgrim, the companion considered himself a peasant called into the presence of a great royal personage.[18] Marjorie calls our gaze back to the crucified

18. Ladinsky, *Love Poems from God,* 207.

and risen Lord, within whose spacious and torn heart all the dimensions of our human experiences can be held and reconciled, for the dilemma that tore her own heart apart was reconciled in a way that made resolution possible as she reminded herself that she was "in Christ."

Marjorie leaves us with the potent reminder that the Cross is the listening post for the pain, wounding, suffering, and seemingly irreconcilable dilemmas that pilgrims bring to their guides and companions. The Cross is our doorway to the kingdom of God.

Conclusion

The Living Flame of Love[1]

O lamps of fire bright-burning
with splendid brilliance, turning
deep caverns of my soul to pools of light!
Once shadowed, dim, unknowing,
now their strange new-found glowing
gives warmth and radiance for my Love's delight.[2]

THE SPACIOUS HEART

THE SPACIOUS heart and inviting spirit of the Master
Companion makes room for all at his banqueting
table. His lamp of fire bright-burning guided the pilgrims
of these pages through the dark interior terrain which the
psalmist calls, "the valley of the shadow of death."[3]

In this concluding chapter, we honor those pilgrims by
speculating about the conversations they might have, if they
were to share about their experiences of healing, forgiveness,

1. John of the Cross, "The Living Flame of Love", 3nd stanza.
Translated by Flower, *Centred on Love*, 22.

2. Ibid., third stanza.

3. Ps 23:4, *NIV*.

and transformation. As they offer one another willing ears
and tender hearts, images, and metaphors punctuate their
speech, drawing them into the silent sanctuary of prayer,
where all that is false is unmasked, and each pilgrim's true
identity and vocation is reflected back "in the face of Jesus
Christ."[4]

In a mysterious way, each pilgrim we companion also
becomes our teacher, offering a gift for our growth as we
are invited into another way of experiencing and perceiving
the world.[5] The vicarious empathy of Christ, who draws us
together, enhances our capacity to enter one another's lives
in this way. As we honor the finitude, estrangements, and
kingdom life experiences of pilgrims, we come closer to all
this within ourselves.

MARTHA AND CAROL: LAMPS OF FIRE
BRIGHT-BURNING

What might Martha talk about with Carol (whom we met
in Chapters Three and Four) if they were to meet at Jesus'
banqueting table? Would she touch on the grief she felt after
her brother, Lazarus, died, and how she told Jesus, "Lord,
if you had been here, my brother would not have died"?[6]
Would she share how she also believed that God would give
Jesus whatever he asked?[7]

Would Carol talk with Martha about the trauma of being an unwanted child? Would she explain how Andrea, her

4. Ringma, *Whispers from the Edge of Eternity,* 107.

5. Oden, *Care of Souls in the Classic Tradition,* 18.

6. John 11:21.

7. John 11:22.

guide-companion, plunged knee-deep into the murky river of her interior and walked beside her, carrying the burning bright lantern of the One who came to heal her deepest wounds and establish her as the beloved daughter of her Heavenly Father?

"Yes, the very same One, who is the resurrection and the life." Martha might reply.

SANDRA AND MARY: TURNING DEEP CAVERNS . . . TO POOLS OF LIGHT

What might Sandra (whom we met in Chapter Seven) talk about with Mary, if they were drawn together around Jesus' banqueting table? Though a committed follower of Jesus who sought to be active in love, there was a shadow side to Sandra's interpersonal work, which led her to believe that she would only receive love if she cared well for others.

Would Sandra perceive that even Mary's spacious, free, and receptive heart became a cavern of darkness and grief after Lazarus's death, when she fell at the feet of Jesus and cried, "Lord, if you had been here, my brother would not have died"?[8] Would Sandra also discern the pain that Mary might have experienced in caring for a weaker family member, as Lazarus might have been disabled or physically weak?

How would Sandra's heart respond to Mary's extravagant gift of love and worship of Jesus? Surely they would share naturally and openly about their love for Jesus, who had transformed their inner wounding and darkness, draw-

8. John 11:32, *NIV.*

ing them into deeper participation in the life of the Trinity, the source of their overflowing love.

DAVID AND LAZARUS: ONCE SHADOWED, DIM, UNKNOWING

A silent, yet very present figure at the banquet table, Lazarus moved from life through death and then back to life again. What mystery lies at the heart of his relationship with the One who raised him from the dead and is now life for him—and for the whole world. Did this quiet man in the background of such miraculous activity grasp his role in the inauguration of the Kingdom of God? Like Lazarus, David (whom we met in Chapter Ten) was plunged into a place of death and darkness as the external scaffolding that had given his life and ministry meaning collapsed, swamping him with an unrelenting flow of destructive thoughts and unrestrained emotions from the shadow side of his long-neglected inner life.

Sitting across from one another at the banquet table, Lazarus and David might find it difficult to bring language to their shared experience of transformation from death to new life. Would David communicate to Lazarus the death-dealing inner struggle that had been his lot for so many days and nights? How might Lazarus describe to David the days he had lain lifeless in the darkness of a cold, closed tomb? Certainly they would find much to talk about regarding the patience of their guide-companions and their capacity to wait until the anointed time to call each forth from his respective grave.

MARJORIE AND THE SAMARITAN WOMAN:
STRANGE NEW-FOUND GLOWING

When we first met the Samaritan woman (in Chapter Five), she was defensive about her story, self-protective because of the ways she'd been wounded and alienated from the people in her community, and constrained to the narrow rim of her existence because of the death-dealing choices she'd made. When she encountered the gentle and humble heart of Jesus, we saw that deep in her being, she was longing to be liberated from her oppressive circumstances and self-loathing.

As Jesus washed her in his forgiving love, grace, and truth, the wounded parts of her innermost being were healed and transformed, and she began the journey towards a resurrected life. This woman, as a fellow recipient of Jesus' healing love, would always be welcome at his banqueting table. And seated next to her, attending thoughtfully and prayerfully to her bubbling enthusiasm and newfound passion for following the Lord, we might not be at all surprised to see the elegant and gracious figure of Marjorie Meyer (whom we met in Chapter Eleven).

The Samaritan woman might share joyfully with Marjorie about the day she went to draw water from Jacob's Well and how her Guide, the Messiah, had invited living water—new life—to bubble up from the very depths of her soul. Love and compassion would undoubtedly light up Marjorie's eyes as she listened to this young woman delight in the love of her Lord. Though her new friend would soon experience the devastating pain of Jesus' death, Marjorie knew that after his resurrection, the Samaritan woman would be liberated into even more abundant life as she trusted in his faithfulness, even amidst suffering and death.

Sitting in the presence of this gentle, wise elder, the Samaritan woman might enquire how Marjorie had nurtured her inner world and would resonate with Marjorie's love of being still and quiet before her Lord.

LOVE'S DELIGHT

Allow our elder pilgrim, Marjorie, with her long life experience of honoring her Love's delight lead you back to the banquet at Bethany, hosted by Mary, Martha, and Lazarus. Sit or stand as close as you can to Jesus, noticing Marjorie as she glances expectantly at Mary, waiting for the moment of anointing that Marjorie has always treasured within her heart. Though Mary's action speaks of death, Marjorie knows that a resurrection morning will follow soon after. Marjorie's own long life has been marked by many such deaths and resurrections, and she thrills at the rapid beating of her heart as she beholds the coming mystery. Her life of untiring service has been Christ's broken bread, her self-giving and other-receiving love his outpoured wine—a fragrant offering poured over the feet of her crucified and risen Lord.[9] Treasure, as would Marjorie, Mary's act of extravagance, abandonment, and freedom. Let it thrill you and cause your heart to race. For this is what it means "to companion in the way of Jesus," and this "reflected love" will guide others into the "Living Flame of Love!"

9. Adapted from Albert Orsborn's hymn, "Christ's Broken Bread." In Coutts, *No Discharge in This War,* 182.

Epilogue

Returning to the Well

IN THIS epilogue, we return to the sacred inner sanctuary of the Samaritan woman after she has begun the journey of transformation into new life. If we obliquely enter this woman's interior, we can imaginatively witness her "soul community" as they experience their Lord's sorrowful entry into Jerusalem, the agony of his death, and his glorious resurrection.

> As he was now approaching the path down from the Mount of Olives, the whole multitude of the disciples began to praise God joyfully with a loud voice for all the deeds of power that they had seen, saying, "Blessed is the king who comes in the name of the Lord! Peace in heaven, and glory in the highest heaven!" Some of the Pharisees in the crowd said to him, "Teacher, order your disciples to stop. He answered, "I tell you, if these were silent, the stones would shout out." As he came near and saw the city, he wept over it, saying, "If you, even you, had only recognized on this day the things that make for peace! But now they are hidden from your eyes. Indeed, the days

> will come upon you, when your enemies will set up ramparts around you and surround you, and hem you in on every side. They will crush you to the ground, you and your children within you, and they will not leave within you one stone upon another; because you did not recognize the time of your visitation from God.[1]

Watchfulness had taken on a most important task in the Samaritan woman's soul community. Each day she would climb the observation tower to scan the horizon for any sight or news of the woman's guide and Lord. There was always much news to share with the others, yet there was a growing concern about the influential religious leaders, who were turning against Jesus.

The day of Jesus' entry into Jerusalem should have been joyous, yet many in the soul community, who had experienced the ecstasy of liberation, now mourned those whose hearts had been hardened. Passion became distraught and lamented, "So many of her kind remained wasted, still struck by the viral numbness."

SORROW AND LOVE FLOW MINGLED DOWN[2]

Jesus' agony in the garden and later, his arrest, trial, and horrific death were darker than any Recollection could remember. Sorrow opened the door to Great Sadness and organized a candlelit vigil for their departed Master. For three whole days, soul's dwelling was shrouded in cold, somber

1. Luke 19:37–44, *NRSV.*

2. From Isaac Watts' Hymn, "When I Survey the Wondrous Cross." In Kendrick, *The Source*, No. 572.

darkness, as every light over the whole earth had been extinguished. All needed a lantern to find the pathway to the observation tower's ladder, where Watchfulness, High Alert, and Recollection took turns standing watch.

LOVE SO AMAZING, SO DIVINE, DEMANDS MY SOUL, MY LIFE, MY ALL.[3]

Watchfulness was on duty well before dawn on the morning of the third day. As she glanced eastward, she discerned a faint light, which intensified into the first beam of the rising sun. A warm breath caressed her cold cheek and penetrated the frozen outer layers of her heart. She reached for the bell cord in a tree hanging just above the observation tower, and its clear, joyful sound pealed throughout the land as the sky continued to brighten. By the time Recollection, Sorrow, and High Alert had climbed the ladder, the horizon was ablaze in golden light.

The One who had brought such liberation to this soul community had died, but now his resurrection launched a new era, indeed a new creation, for the whole world. The members of the soul community gathered in a great circle and wove the golden threads they'd been given by their Master into a single, long cord. The fire in their hearts burned, and every face shone like the sun.

At Praise's signal, they broke into a song of jubilation and thanksgiving: Hallelujah, Hallelujah, Hallelujah!, a refrain that echoed back from the furthest ends of the earth and beyond heaven's realms.

3. Ibid.

Afterword

IN THESE pages we have been able to enter the encounters between pilgrims and those who companion them on the journey. Whether these companions are counselors, pastors, chaplains or spiritual directors, they open a place of heart-listening in the Way of Jesus. The Way of Jesus is not primarily psychological, directive or even using good listening skills. It is a Way of bringing the whole of the human person, in the presence of the living God, to the service of the pilgrim. In this relationship of reflected love, the soul life of both companion and pilgrim is awakened and enlivened, offering possibilities of newness—in both identity and vocation. Jesus' Way is a way of bringing a gentle and humble heart to be present to the fragile heart of the other, in the presence of the wounded heart of God.

Companion guides are invited to look more deeply in the way Jesus is present to those he companions—accepting their fragility, reactivity, and woundedness, and opening a hospitable space which bids all of the parts of the person to come and find rest.

As I have watched Chris relating over the last twelve years—both in the classroom, the counseling or spiritual direction context, and with myself, I have been able to observe a new and different way of being with the other, the heart beat of his way of companioning which has several interactive dimensions. I have been struck by how quickly pilgrims are drawn to the deeper places of their being, how often they are quickly in tears. "How does he do that?" I have asked. The answer is partly what Chris himself brings to the relationship. His own journey into darkness and pain in the company of the Master Companion, enables him to go towards those places in the other. As in Carol's gentle but intentional companioning in chapter 3, Chris consistently stays with the pain of the other. It is his own journey with pain that enables him to not shy away from it. This makes it possible for the pilgrim to be held present to their own pain, but kept safe by the presence of one who understands, and is not afraid.

The students we have worked with over the years continue to talk of the golden thread. They have themselves learned to listen to the deeper places of their own hearts to intuit and respond to the golden thread of grace that works its way through the pilgrim's story. As they learn to attune their own hearts to inklings of pain and darkness, as they walk through their own journeys of wounding and reaction, they become more receptive to these places in the lives of pilgrims, and more able to stay in the dark places with them, trusting that the One who is already present will bring rest to the soul. They learn to give sensitive response to the pilgrims' concerns creating a space for deeper reflection, so they can name their own metaphors, identify the threads of their own story, and find their own knowing of God.

As I have observed Chris's practice I have also seen him develop in his expression of the Way of Jesus. His knowing of the One who empties himself, who goes to the place of pain, and who knows the pattern of life-death-life has enabled him to journey with others in a way that brings them more intentionally to the One whose presence heals. It is not that Chris introduces God into the encounter explicitly, but he himself is in a place of prayer, listening attentively for both the movement of the Spirit, and the awareness of pilgrims to their own spirituality. Chris often waits as Stephen did in chapter 10, until the other mentions God. Or he may ask, as Amy did in chapter 7, "Who could help?" It is only when the pilgrim mentions God that Chris responds, holding sacred the journey that the person is making, and trusting the Holy Spirit to guide both himself and the pilgrim. When the person is ready to turn their gaze to God, then the guide can gently hold that space, witness to an encounter with the living and present Christ.

Reflected Love is an exploration of the Way of Jesus, the way each guide may find his or her own way to journey with others, to hold the pilgrims' anxieties, fears, and pain, following the gentle and humble heart of him who came to give us life—in all its abundance.

Irene Alexander
Easter 2011

Bibliography

Bourgeault, Cynthia. *Centering Prayer and Inner Awakening.* Cambridge Massachusetts: Cowley Publications, 2004.

Brown, Christopher. "Dismantling the walls that divide." *Zadok Paper* S78 (Summer 1996), 1–14.

Coutts, Frederick. *No Discharge in This War.* London: Hodder & Stoughton, 1975.

Davis, Noel. *Fallow's Hundredfold.* Sydney: Shekinah Creative Centre, 2000.

Dillard, Annie. *Pilgrim at Tinker Creek.* New York: Harper Collins, 1998.

Green, Thomas. *Opening to God: A Guide to Prayer.* Indiana: Ave Maria Press, 1977.

Hillesum, Etty and Eva Hoffman. *Etty Hillesum: An Interrupted Life the Diaries.1941–1943 and Letters from Westerbork.* New York: Henry Holt, 1996.

Jinkins, Michael. *Invitation to Theology: A Guide to Study, Conversation & Practice.* Illinois: IVP Academic, 2001.

John of the Cross. "The Living Flame of Love." In *Centred on Love: The Poems of St John of the Cross.* Translated by Marjorie Flower OCD. Varroville: Carmelite Nuns, 2002.

Kendrick, Graham. *The Source.* Suffolk: Kevin Mayhew, 1998.

Ladinsky, Daniel. *Love Poems from God.* New York: Penguin Compass, 2002.

Laird, Martin. *Into the Silent Land: The Practice of Contemplation.* London: Darton, Longman and Todd, 2006.

Lawrence, Brother. *The Practice of the Presence of God.* Grand Rapids: Spire, 1967.

Manton, Karen. *The Gift of Julian of Norwich.* Melbourne, VIC: John Garratt, 2005.

McDonnell, Thomas. editor. *A Merton Reader*. New York: Image Books, 1989.

Nicholson D. H. S. and A. H. E. Lee. editors. *The Oxford Book of English Mystical Verse*. Oxford: The Clarendon Press, 1917.

Oden, Thomas. *Care of Souls in the Classic Tradition*. Philadelphia: Fortress Press, 1984.

O'Donohue, John. *Eternal Echoes*. New York: HarperCollins, 1999.

Peterson, Eugene. *Leap Over a Wall: Earthy Spirituality for Everyday Christians*. New York: HarperOne, 1997.

Peterson, Eugene. *The Message*. Colorado: Navpress, 1993.

Quiller-Couch, Arthur. editor. *The Oxford Book of English Verse 1250–1900*. Oxford: Clarendon, 1919.

Ringma, Charles. *Whispers from the Edge of Eternity*. Vancouver: Regent, 2005.

Rogers, Carl. *Carl Rogers on Personal Power*. New York: Delacorte Press, 1977.

Sampson, John. editor. *The Poems of William Blake*. London: Senate, 1995.

Shakespeare, William. *Hamle*t, 1601.

Shaw, Luci. *Widening Light: Poems on the Incarnation*. Vancouver: Harold Shaw, 1984.

The Methodist Hymn Book. London: Methodist Conference Office. Aylesbury: Hazell, Watson & Viney Ltd, 1933.

van Kaam, Adrian and Susan Muto. *Dynamics of Spiritual Direction*. Pittsburgh: Epiphany, 2003.

Volf, Miroslav. *Exclusion and Embrace: A Theological Exploration of Identity, Otherness, and Reconciliation*. Nashville: Abingdon Press, 1996.

von Goethe, Johann Wolfgang. *Goethe's Faust*. Translated by Walter Kaufmann. New York: Random House, 1961.

Wordsworth, William. *Poetical Works*. Oxford: Oxford University, 1904.